Easy English!

Series Editor

Adrian Wallwork
English for Academics SAS
Pisa, Italy

Easy English is a series of books intended for students and teachers of English as a foreign language.

More information about this series at http://www.springer.com/series/15586

Adrian Wallwork

Test Your Personality

Have Fun and Learn Useful Phrases

Adrian Wallwork
English for Academics SAS
Pisa, Italy

ISSN 2522-8617 ISSN 2522-8625 (electronic)
Easy English!
ISBN 978-3-319-67225-0 ISBN 978-3-319-67226-7 (eBook)
https://doi.org/10.1007/978-3-319-67226-7

Library of Congress Control Number: 2017963150

© Springer International Publishing AG 2018
This work is subject to copyright. All rights are reserved by the Publisher, whether the whole or part of the material is concerned, specifically the rights of translation, reprinting, reuse of illustrations, recitation, broadcasting, reproduction on microfilms or in any other physical way, and transmission or information storage and retrieval, electronic adaptation, computer software, or by similar or dissimilar methodology now known or hereafter developed.
The use of general descriptive names, registered names, trademarks, service marks, etc. in this publication does not imply, even in the absence of a specific statement, that such names are exempt from the relevant protective laws and regulations and therefore free for general use.
The publisher, the authors and the editors are safe to assume that the advice and information in this book are believed to be true and accurate at the date of publication. Neither the publisher nor the authors or the editors give a warranty, express or implied, with respect to the material contained herein or for any errors or omissions that may have been made. The publisher remains neutral with regard to jurisdictional claims in published maps and institutional affiliations.

Printed on acid-free paper

This Springer imprint is published by Springer Nature
The registered company is Springer International Publishing AG
The registered company address is: Gewerbestrasse 11, 6330 Cham, Switzerland

Student's Introduction

What Is *Easy English*?

Easy English is a series of books to help you learn and revise your English with minimal effort. You can improve your English by

- reading texts in English that you might well normally read in your own language e.g. personality tests (this book), jokes, lateral thinking games, wordsearches.
- doing short exercises to improve specific areas grammar and vocabulary, i.e. the areas that tend to lead to the most mistakes - the aim is just to focus on what you really need rather than overwhelming yourself with a mass of rules, many of which may have no practical daily value

What Level of English Do I Need in Order to Benefit from this Book?

If your level is intermediate (B2) and above, then you should be able to do the vast majority of the tests, particularly if you make use of the glossaries that precede them.

How Will this Book Help Me Improve My English?

The aim of this series is to enable you to do something you would have done in your own language and can have fun doing in English.

One benefit of personality tests is that they are generally short without any big blocks of text. This means that they are relatively quick and easy to read. They also contain a considerable amount of vocabulary that is is typical of everyday conversation, but that you may not have met during English lessons or reading English language coursebooks.

Use of *They, Them* as Generic Pronouns

In this book the pronouns *they, them* and occasionally *themself* are used as an alternative to *him/her* and *themselves* For example:
   A good friend of yours is at home with flu. Would you:

a) Go and visit **them** immediately?
b) Wait a couple of days before visiting **them**?

In the above case, *a good friend* is singular and refers to just one person. However, the gender/sex of this person is not important. In such cases the third person plural pronoun - *they, them, their* - is used. This usage is considered ungrammatical by some, but is both useful and commonly used (and has been for centuries).

How Seriously Should I Take the Scores and the Explanations of the Personality Traits?

This book is NOT intended to be an amateur psychology book or self-help book. Neither the quizzes nor the explanations should be taken any more seriously than you would take a horoscope in a newspaper or magazine.
   These quizzes were designed primarily to enable you to:

- learn some useful English vocabulary
- have fun doing something in English that you might equally well have done in your own language

The quizzes themselves are fairly light-hearted. The explanations of the personality traits, on the other hand, are often (but not always) considerably more serious.
   I had the choice of providing very frivolous superficial explanations or providing explanations that were to some extent pseudo-psychological. I preferred the latter solution simply because it provided considerably more scope for vocabulary learning. The result is, on occasions, a bit of dichotomy between the lightness of the quiz and the heaviness of the explanations.
   So should you take the quizzes and explanations seriously?
   No!

What Should I Do if I Don't Understand Some of the Words in the Quiz or the Explanation?

Before each quiz there is a list of words (glossary) that you might be unfamiliar plus their definitions. Note: These definitions are for the word as it is used in the particular context of the joke. All the words marked in *italics* in the main text are in the glossary.

If the word you don't know is not in the glossary or if there are words in the definitions that you don't understand, then try using context.reverso.com to see the word used in context and the various translations into your own language.

Alternatively do a Google search. In the search box simply type in the word followed by 'definition'. This will automatically generate a definition. You will need to choose the definition that best matches the context of the quiz/explanation.

You can also hear the pronunciation of the word by clicking on the sound icon - both for Google and context. reverso.

How Should I Use the Glossaries?

The glossaries at the beginning of each chapter list some of the words that you may not know in the main text (i.e. the tests and scores/interpretations). They are listed in the order that they appear in the text. In the text they are written in *italics*.

Note: The glossaries only contain the definition of the word/phrase as used within the context of the joke.

You can use them to:

- check whether you remember the meanings of the words of phrases. To do this, simply cover the right-hand column
- use the white space at the end of each definition in order to write down the translation of the word/phrase

How Should I Use the Vocabulary Exercises at the End of the Book?

The vocabulary exercises are based on the glossaries for each chapter. The exercise is simple: match the terms with their definitions.

If you complete these exercises, your knowledge of colloquial (rather than technical, financial or academic English) will improve considerably.

What Are the Other Books in this Series? Which One Should I Read Next?

Currently there are six books in the series.

Test your personality - *have fun and learn useful phrases*
Wordsearches - *widen your vocabulary in English*
Word games, riddles and logic tests - *tax your brain and boost your English*
Jokes - *have a laugh and improve your English*
Top 50 grammar mistakes in English - *how to avoid them*
Top 50 vocabulary mistakes in English - *how to avoid them*

These books are designed to be dipped into rather than being read from the first page to the last. 'Dipped into' means that you can pick up the book and read any page you like, and for as long as you like.

You are likely to have more fun with the books if you read two or three at the same time. So rather than spending the next month reading personality tests, you might find it more fun and stimulating to read a few jokes one day, and do a few wordsearches.

Teacher's Introduction

Why Personality Tests?

Personality tests are ubiquitous in magazines and on the web. Native English speakers love them. So do non-natives. In fact, personality tests are often used in coursebooks and workbooks in the world of EFL. However, as far as I am aware, there are no collections of personality tests used for self-study by non-native speakers or in the classroom.

What Type of Students Would the Tests Work Well with?

The majority of tests are only suitable for adults. A few, i.e. those discussing relationships with friends, family and attitudes to risks, would also be suitable for teenagers.

The ones in Chapters 9, 10 and 11, which are all work-related, would work well with students doing business English or in-house company courses.

All would be suitable for adults doing general English courses, with an upper intermediate level and above.

How Seriously Should My Students Take the Tests and the Related Scores?

The tests should absolutely NOT be taken seriously.

They are simply designed as an interesting read, a means of learning some new vocabulary and expressions (of the kind that don't usually come up in an English lesson), and, if used in the classroom, as a springboard for discussion.

Some of the tests and scores are quite frivolous, others much more serious - this was deliberate in order to allow me to introduce different types of vocabulary with different registers. But whatever the case, students should be made aware that they are just for fun.

How Can I Use the Tests in the Class?

Before you use a test for the first time with a class, have a class discussion on

- what a personality test is
- where they are typically found (magazines, self-help books, on the web)
- whether the students do/like such tests
- how seriously such tests should be taken

Make it very clear that the tests that you will be giving them should not be taken seriously but merely as a springboard for discussion.

You can use the personality tests as:

- a warm up
- as a filler
- as a discussion exercise

They require almost zero preparation on your part. The vocabulary to pre-teach is listed in the glossaries. You can then proceed as follows:

1. students complete the test individually or in pairs
2. they check their score
3. in pairs or groups, students compare and discuss their answers, and then discuss whether they agree with the score. This could then lead on to a wider discussion of the topic in question

There are also other approaches in which the personality test becomes the key point of the whole lesson. Here is an idea you might like to try out:

1. give students the title of the test, without giving them the test itself
2. in pairs, students have to think of three or four questions/topics that they think might appear in the test
3. students compare their questions with another group, and choose what they consider to be the best four, or the four most likely to appear in the test
4. hand out the test
5. students do the test, see how many of their questions/topics were covered
6. discussion on whose questions were the best - the ones in the test or the ones they invented themselves

The above procedure will really motivate the students to do the test and read the questions carefully.

Teacher's Introduction

What Should I Do About any Unfamiliar Vocabulary?

The aim of this book is to teach students vocab that is unlikely to come up spontaneously during your lessons or appear in the coursebooks that you use. It is 'authentic' vocabulary taken from personality tests, the vast majority of which were designed for native English speakers rather than foreign learners.

So your students will be reading the 'real thing', with all the advantages and disadvantages that this implies.

At the beginning of each test there is a glossary with definitions that refer to the meaning of the word or phrase within the context of the test. The definitions are 'authentic' too, meaning that they also may contain vocabulary that your students are unfamiliar with.

For any words that your students can't work out from the context or from the glossaries I suggest you get your students to search for them on context.reverso.net. This wonderful website shows the key word used in context along with a translation into the student's own language. It gives many many examples, so students should be able to find the context that matches the text that they are reading.

Where Did the Tests Come from?

In the Sources & Acknowledgements at the end of this introduction, you can see the main sources for the quizzes. You will note that they are all books from the 1980s and 1990s, virtually all of which are now out of print and/or which score over 5,000,000 in the Amazon Bestsellers Rank.

The reason for this choice was to provide teachers and students with materials that they would be unable to find elsewhere.

Possibly the most interesting part of writing this book was actually reading the original quizzes, and how much of the content would be simply unacceptable today. The role of women, or at least our perception of the role of women, has changed considerably since the books were published. Many personality tests of that era were based on incredible stereotypes of men's and women's roles, and often the the pronoun *he* was used in a generic way. With my wife, Anna Southern, we have tried to remove all such 'archaic' questions, and have thus 'modernized' the questions for readers of the 2020s!

Other tests were taken from various magazines that I have collected over 35 years of my career in TEFL, and many questions I have invented myself.

Any feedback on the choice of tests, the wording and the scoring would be much appreciated.

What Other Similar Books Might I Find Useful?

If you teach children and young teenagers, they you might be interested in my book of word games called *Mindtwisters* (published by Scholastic).

Various games and discussion exercises (including various quizzes/personality tests) for older teenagers and adults can be found in *Discussions AZ* (two volumes: intermediate and advanced, published by Cambridge University Press).

There is also a series of discussion, warm up exercises, fillers etc published by SEFL (sefl.co.uk).

Ideas for Other Books for this Series

If you have any ideas for other books that could be part of the *Easy English* series then please email me.

The Author

Since 1984 Adrian Wallwork has been teaching English as a foreign language - from General English to Business English to Scientific English. Although he lives and works in Pisa (Italy), through his university work he has taught students of all nationalities. Adrian is the author of over 30 textbooks for Springer Science+Business Media, Cambridge University Press, Oxford University Press, the BBC, and many other publishers. He can be contacted at: adrian.wallwork@gmail.com

Sources & Acknowledgements

Some questions and scores in some of the quizzes were based on questions and scores taken from the following books:

a) Know Your Own Mind, James Green & David Lewis, Penguin, 1988
b) On The Spot, Albie Fiore, Penguin, 1986
c) Pulling Your Own Strings, Wayne W Dyer, Hamlyn, 1978
d) Strengthen your Performance in Psychological Tests, Cecile Cesari, Foulsham, 1996
e) Test Yourself, William Bernard & Jules Leopold, Corgi, 1986
f) The Book of Tests, Michael Nathenson, Fontana, 1984
g) The Personality Test, Peter Lauster, Chilton Book Company, 1976
h) Your Personality Quiz Book, Glenn Wilson, Hodder&Stoughton, 1994

I also took questions and scores from an insert published by the Sunday Times in the early 1980s and entitled:

i) Lifeplan Scorechart

The following tests (numbers in bold) were adapted from a previously published quiz. The letters refer to the books listed above:
3 c, **5** h, **11** c, **13** i, **38** f, **40** e, **41** i,
Test 2 was originally compiled by Suzanne Thomas.
Test 47 was adapted from 'Conducting Effective Meetings' in Effective Meetings, Marion E. Haynes, Kogan Page, 1988

I would like to thank Anna Southern for sifting through the vast quantities of materials I produced for this book and for weeding out the dross, the politically incorrect, and the downright absurd. Particular thanks to Robert Parks at Wordsmyth and Prabhav Jain at EasyDefine, who gave me permission to use the definitions automatically generated by their website. EasyDefine definitions are taken from https://wordnet.princeton.edu/wordnet/citing-wordnet/

Contents

1	**General Traits**		1
	1	Are you an Extrovert or an Introvert?	1
	2	Are You an Optimist or a Pessimist?	4
	3	Are You a Victor or a Victim?	7
	4	Are You a Confident or an Anxious Person?	11
	5	Are You a Morning or an Evening Person?	14
2	**Risks and Sensations**		17
	6	Do You Like Taking Risks?	17
	7	Are You a Sensation Seeker?	21
	8	How Cautious Are You?	24
	9	How Spontaneous Are You?	27
	10	What Is Your Attitude Towards Driving and Drivers?	29
3	**Confidence Levels**		33
	11	Are You Assertive?	33
	12	How Easily Do You Get Embarrassed?	33
	13	How Strong Is Your Personality?	34
	14	How Confident Are You?	34
	15	How Much Do You Like To Be in the Spotlight?	34
4	**Trust, Honesty, Altruism and Ambition**		43
	16	How Trusting and Trustworthy Are You?	43
	17	How Honest Are You?	46
	18	How Altruistic Are You?	49
	19	How Nice Are You?	52
	20	How Tactful Are You?	54
	21	How Ambitious Are You?	57

5 Health and Body ... 59
- 22 How Healthy Are You? ... 59
- 23 How Happy Are You With Yourself? ... 59
- 24 How Happy Are You With Your Body? ... 60
- 25 How Obsessed Are You About Your Job? ... 60
- 26 Are You a Victim of Stress? ... 60

6 Image, Imagination and Communication ... 67
- 27 How Important Are Personal Image and Ambition for You? ... 67
- 28 How Imaginative Are You? ... 68
- 29 How Do You Communicate? ... 70
- 30 How Strong Are Your Psychic Powers? ... 72
- 31 To What Extent Do You Live in Your Own Dream World? ... 74

7 Friends' Family and Partners ... 77
- 32 What Kind of a Friend Are You? ... 77
- 33 What Do You Look For in a Partner? ... 77
- 34 How Well Does Your Partner Know You and Do You Know Your Partner? ... 78
- 35 How Well Do Your Family Know You? ... 78
- 36 What Kind of a Parent Are You (Would You Be)? ... 78

8 Logic and Reasoning ... 87
- 37 Are You a Logical Thinker? ... 87
- 38 Do You Think With Your Right Brain or Left Brain? ... 89
- 39 How Versatile Are You? ... 91
- 40 How Responsible Are Your Decisions? ... 93
- 41 How Well Do You Handle Your Finances? ... 95

9 Work ... 97
- 42 What Kind of Job Would You Like? ... 97
- 43 What Do You Want From a Job? ... 98
- 44 What Kind of Job Would You Prefer? ... 98
- 45 You and Your Job ... 98
- 46 Should You Change Job? ... 98

10 Effectiveness in Work Environment ... 107
- 47 Do You Have Effective Meeting Skills? ... 107
- 48 Are You a Good Negotiator? ... 107
- 49 How Well Do You Manage Your Time? ... 108
- 50 Are You a Risk Taker? ... 108
- 51 How Ethical Are You? ... 108

11	**Managerial Skills**		117
	52	Do You Have Managerial Potential?	117
	53	Would You Be an Ethical Leader?	117
	54	Would You Make a Good Manager?	118
	55	How Well Does Your Boss Know You?	118
	56	Do You Have a Manager's Approach to Work?	118
12	**Miscellaneous**		125
	57	What Are Your Daily Habits?	125
	58	How Mature Are You?	126
	59	Are You Caught in the Web?	126
	60	Are You a Sensible Shopper?	126
	61	What Class of Airplane Passenger Are You?	126

Appendix 1 135
Appendix 2 147
Index 163

Chapter 1
General Traits

1 Are you an Extrovert or an Introvert?

Glossary

hike - *v.* go for a long walk for exercise or pleasure

day dream - *n.* dream during the day, e.g. thoughts about things you'd like to do, or places where you'd like to be, or people you'd like to be with

decorating - *n.* painting and furnishing your house / flat / room

pointless - *adj.* serving no useful purpose

stuff - *n.* miscellaneous unspecified objects

clapping - *n.* a demonstration of approval by repeatedly putting your hands together to make a noise

exotic - *adj.* strikingly strange or unusual; characteristic of another place or part of the world

outgoing - *adj.* extrovert, at ease in talking to others

spot - *v.* notice, identify

life and soul - *n.* the center of attention / energy at a social event

energize - *v.* inject with energy

aware - *adj.* having or showing knowledge or understanding; conscious; attentive to

alienate - *v.* arouse indifference or hostility where there had previously been harmony, understanding, affection, or friendliness

energy draining - *adj.* lowering your levels of energy

continuum - *n.* succession in which no one part is distinct or distinguishable from another

1 Are You an Extrovert or an Introvert?

Choose the answer - a) or b) - that is most similar to your personality.

1. I like to read books about

   a people like myself
   b great people and adventurers

2. I prefer sports such as

   a football, basketball and other team sports
   b cycling, tennis, *hiking*, skiing and other more individual sports

3. I would rather join

   a a political or social club
   b an organization dedicated to literature or science

4. I like to wear clothes that

   a stress my individuality
   b are quite similar to everyone else's

5. My *daydreams* mostly consist of me

   a building/*decorating* my dream home
   b on holiday on a Caribbean island

6. Keeping a diary for me

   a would be a useful exercise
   b would be *pointless* - I like to share *stuff* directly with my friends

7. Coffee breaks at work are for employees to have

   a a chance to get to know each other better
   b time to relax a bit so that they can be more efficient when they get back to their desks

8. When on public transport I

   a try to engage in conversation with someone sitting near me
   b play on my mobile phone

9. At the end of a concert

   a I am usually one of the last people to stop *clapping*
   b I finish clapping before most of the rest of the audience

10. Most of the pictures I have on Instagram and Facebook are

    a various generations of family and friends
    b me in various *exotic* places

SCORE

Extroverts tend to answer yes to the following questions:

1) b 2) a 3) a 4) a 5) b 6) b 7) a 8) a 9) a 10) b

Introverts tend to answer yes to the following questions:

1) a 2) b 3) b 4) b 5) c 6) a 7) b 8) b 9) b 10) a

EXTROVERTS

If you choose seven or more answers typical of extroverts, then you basically have an extrovert personality. The Oxford English Dictionary defines an extrovert as an *outgoing* and socially confident person, and as a person who is predominantly concerned with external things or objective considerations. You can *spot* an extrovert as they are likely to be the one who is the *life and soul* at a social gathering. They're ones who do most of the talking. Their friendly and positive enthusiasm tends to make people enjoy their company. They need other people around them and are *energized* by such social contact. If you are an extrovert, be *aware* of the fact your exuberance and constant talking may actually *alienate* some people.

INTROVERTS

If you choose seven or more answers typical of introverts, then you basically have an introvert personality. The Oxford English Dictionary defines an introvert as being shy and reticent, a person who is predominantly concerned with their own thoughts and feelings, rather than with external things. Three typical signs that you are an introvert: i) you have a small group of close friends; ii) you prefer not being around a lot of people at the same time and find it *energy draining*; iii) and other people describe you as being quiet or even difficult to get to know.

MIDDLE GROUND

If you scored five or six on either for the extrovert or introvert answers, then you are somewhere in the middle of the extroversion-introversion *continuum*. While many introverts will be socially reserved and would prefer to stay home and read a book rather than go to a party, but there are many so-called introverts who enjoy socializing.

2 Are You an Optimist or a Pessimist?

Glossary

lovely - *adj.* beautiful, very nice

cardigan - *n.* knitted jacket that is fastened up the front with buttons or a zipper

presume - *v.* accept without verification or proof

praise - *v.* express approval of

assignment - *n.* exercise, task, essay

resign yourself - *v.* accept as inevitable

ask someone out - *v.* find out whether someone is interested in going out for a drink, going to the cinema with you etc.

flu - *n.* common and contagious viral disease (short form of 'influenza')

application - *n.* request for employment or admission to a school/college

overqualified *adj.* with more than a sufficient number of qualifications and thus probably unsuitable/unsuited to a particular job

come out on top - *v.* get very good results, better than others

crop up - *v.* take place, occur, happen

glide - *v.* move smoothly and effortlessly

unscathed - *adj.* completely unharmed

a pot of gold - *n.* a container full of gold found at in folklore is reputedly found at the end of a rainbow

rainbow - *n.* an arc of colored light in the sky

cheery - *adj.* bright and pleasant; promoting a feeling of cheer

(look on the) bright side of life - *exp.* always see the positive aspects of a situation

get someone down - *v.* disappoint, make sad/depressed

(be at the) back of your mind - *exp.* a feeling or thought that is constantly with you

turn / work out right - *exp.* have a final positive result

chuckle - *v.* laugh quietly or with restraint

be dealt a bad hand - *exp.* be given a series of negative factors to deal with

cheer up - *v.* become more content after being sad

2 Are You an Optimist or a Pessimist?

Choose the most appropriate answer for yourself.

1. The weather forecast says it's going to be a *lovely* summer's day. Do you:

    a Smile and put on a T shirt?
    b Put a T shirt on, and put a *cardigan* in your bag?
    c Take an umbrella?

2. You ask a friend a favor. Do you:

    a Automatically assume they will agree?
    b Think there's a 50% chance they will be OK about it?
    c *Presume* that you are probably wasting your time?

Depending on your situation (student or employee) answer just one of the following two questions (3A or 3B).

3A Student: Your professor asks you to stay behind at the end of a lesson. Do you:

    a Think they are going to *praise* you about your last written *assignment*?
    b Remain calm because you know it can't be anything serious?
    c Prepare yourself for a major criticism of your work?

3B Employee: Your boss asks you to come to their desk. Do you:

    a Think they are going to *praise* you about your work on a recently finished project?
    b Remain calm because you know it can't be anything serious?
    c Prepare yourself for a major criticism of your work?

4. You've been going out with your partner for three months. For three days you haven't heard from them. Do you:

    a Think they must have had some kind of emergency?
    b Feel sure they will contact you within the next 12 hours?
    c Realise that they must have found someone else?

5. If you started a course/job that you hated, would you:

    a Leave after a day?
    b Try it out for three months?
    c *Resign* yourself to the fact that there's nothing you can do about it?

6. Someone you have liked for several years has two tickets for a concert. Would you:

   a Think 'finally he/she is going to *ask me out*'?
   b Think nothing in particular?
   c Assume that everyone else that they could have asked is busy?

7. A good friend of yours is at home with *flu*. Would you:

   a Go and visit them immediately?
   b Wait a couple of days before visiting them?
   c Stay away?

8. Someone who you've not been in contact with suddenly phones you. Do you:

   a Expect to hear some great news?
   b Answer the call because you are curious to know why they are ringing you?
   c Assume something tragic must have happened?

9. You send in an *application* for a course/job. The application is refused. Do you assume that:

   a You were probably *overqualified*?
   b You simply weren't good enough?
   c They hated your photo on your CV?

10. You have organized a dinner party. Would you expect your guests to:

    a Arrive early?
    b Arrive a little late?
    c Send an sms to say they can't come?

SCORE
PREDOMINANTLY A'S

You didn't really need to do this test - you knew you would *come out on top*. You manage to stay happy whatever happens. Even when problems do *crop up*, you seem to *glide* through *unscathed*. You are the type of person that expects *a pot of gold* at the end of a *rainbow* - and usually finds it.

PREDOMINANTLY B'S

You're *cheery* and look on the *bright side of life* most of the time. But, like most people, the big problems *get you down*. Yet, *in the back of your mind*, there is always something telling you that it will *turn out right in the end*. You can usually manage to *chuckle* over some of your misfortunes - at least when they're over.

PREDOMINANTLY C'S

Oh dear! Life is just one rainy day after another for you, isn't it? You can't seem to step out of bed in the morning without imagining some hopeless disaster cropping up. You tend to feel that life has *dealt you a bad hand*, and that nothing will ever *work out* right. *Cheer up* - things can't get any worse.

3 Are You a Victor or a Victim?

Glossary

elderly - *adj.* advanced in years

bloated - *adj.* with a very full stomach

blame - *v.* attribute the responsibility to someone for something that has gone wrong

be in a hurry - *v.* have a very limited amount of time

moaner - *n.* a person given to excessive complaints and crying

resign yourself - *v.* accept as inevitable

up to scratch - *adj.* of expected quality

succumb - *v.* consent reluctantly

(to be) supposed to - *v.* to be expected to

(to be) overcharged - *v.* to pay more than was due or expected

well done - *adj.* cooked for a sufficient time to remove the redness (blood) of the meat

medium-rare - *adj.* cooked a little, quite a bit of blood is left

gift - *n.* a present

bark - *v.* the loud noise made by a dog

ear plugs - *n.* device to put in your ears to stop external sound from penetrating your ears

enrolled - *adj.* registered

turn out - *v.* reveal itself to be

ineffectual - *adj.* lacking in power or forcefulness

sit out - *v.* remain for the whole duration

prying - *adj.* too curious or inquisitive

perceived - *adj.* detected by instinct or inference

failure - *n.* the opposite of success

lack - *v.* be without

boundary - *n.* limit

self esteem - *n.* an attitude of admiration, approval and liking of and for oneself

shyness - *n.* a feeling of fear of embarrassment

set yourself up - *v.* allow yourself to be in a weak position so that someone else can potentially do something negative to you

sympathy - *n.* sharing and understanding the negative feelings or situation of others

3 Are You a Victor or a Victim?

Task 1: Decide which of the two options you would normally follow in your own life.
Task 2: For each pair of options, decide which is the victim response.

1. Your *elderly* aunt calls you on the phone at a very busy moment.

    a You patiently listen to what she has to say.
    b You ask her to ring back at a more convenient time.

2. You are eating dinner at someone's house. You are full although you haven't finished everything on your plate.

    a You stop eating the moment you don't feel hungry anymore.
    b You finish what's on your plate even though this leaves you feeling *bloated*.

3. You've been *blamed* for misplacing something, which in fact you've never touched.

    a You help in trying to find the misplaced object.
    b You ignore the accusation and carry on with what you are doing.

4. You are in a hurry at the supermarket. All the queues are very long.

    a You explain that you are in a *hurry* and ask someone if you can go to the front of the queue.
    b You wait your turn.

5. A habitual *moaner* starts complaining to you about their life.

    a You listen to what they have to say.
    b You tell them life's too short and make an excuse and leave.

6. You are in a two-star hotel and the air conditioning in your room doesn't work.

    a You immediately phone reception.
    b You *resign yourself* to the fact that the room didn't cost much.

7. The food you've just had in a restaurant is not *up to scratch* and the service has been inadequate.

    a You pay the optional service charge on the bill.
    b You inform the management of your dissatisfaction.

8. Your partner's friend always kisses you when they greet you. You don't like being kissed by this person.

    a You extend your hand and keep your face away.
    b You *succumb* to the kiss.

9. At work someone asks you to do a task that they are *supposed to do* themselves.

    a You politely refuse.
    b You do what they ask.

10. You have been slightly *overcharged* at a shop.

    a You say nothing - what's a few cents?
    b You bring it to the sales assistant's attention.

11. You have an outside table at a restaurant. Someone on the next table starts smoking.

    a You ask them not to smoke.
    b You try to keep your face away from the smoke that is blowing directly at you.

12. At a restaurant you ask for your steak to be *well done*. The steak arrives *medium-rare*.

    a You eat it.
    b You send it back.

13. Someone who you lent $10 to still hasn't paid you back.

    a You remind them.
    b You *resign* yourself to the fact that it is unlikely you will ever see the money again.

14. You are on a diet imposed by your doctor. At a friend's house they offer you a piece of their birthday cake.

    a You eat a small piece.
    b You say 'no thank you'.

15. You order a soft drink at a restaurant. The drink arrives but two thirds of the glass is ice.

    a You ask for another glass with much less ice.
    b You say nothing.

16. A work colleague invites you to their party and you are expected to buy them a present whether you go or not. You don't want to go.

    a You give them a *gift* at work, but don't go to the party.
    b No gift, no party.

17. One of your neighbor's dogs *barks* loudly at 5 o'clock every morning.

    a You buy *ear plugs*.
    b In the evening you go to the neighbor and explain that the situation has become intolerable.

18. You *enrolled* on a course held by what *turns out* to be an *ineffectual* and poorly-prepared professor.

    a You *sit out* the course.
    b You abandon the course.

19. You are out for dinner with friends. At the end of the meal the waiter gives you the bill.

   a You calculate how much each person owes and tell them.
   b You pay the bill yourself.

20. Someone is *prying* into your private life by preceding questions with "I know perhaps I shouldn't be asking, but …"

   a You tell them what they want to hear.
   b You tell them to mind their own business.

ANSWERS AND SCORE

VICTOR

1) b 2) a 3) b 4) a 5) b 6) a 7) b 8) a 9) a 10) b 11) a 12) b 13) a 14) b 15) a 16) b 17) b 18) b 19) a 20) b

If you gave more than 15 victor answers then you rarely regard yourself as being the victim of the negative actions of others, as you realise there is clear evidence that such actions were only *perceived* by you as being negative and that this perception is due to habitual thought processes. Instead, you learned in childhood not to be a victim and to be responsible for your own actions - both successes and *failures*.

VICTIM

1) a 2) b 3) a 4) b 5) a 6) b 7) a 8) b 9) b 10) a 11) b 12) a 13) b 14) a 15) b 16) a 17) a 18) a 19) b 20) a

If you gave more than 10 victim answers then you probably have many of the following characteristics. You *lack* self-confidence and are easily influenced by others. You have some difficulty in communicating with others and in establishing and maintaining *boundaries*. Because of your low level of *self esteem* and high level of *shyness* you find it hard to say no (you basically want to please everyone). You may or may not be *setting yourself up* to be a target of victimization, and you may or may not be eliciting the *sympathy* of those around you, but whatever the situation you need to learn to have more confidence in yourself and take more responsibility for your own actions and feelings.

4 Are You a Confident or an Anxious Person?

Glossary

shaking - *v.* when your body moves involuntarily when something negative has happened to you or is about to happen

trembling - *v.* slight shaking

nightmare - *n.* bad/unpleasant dream

cheer yourself up - *v.* make yourself feel better after a negative event

miserable - *adj.* very unhappy

harmless - *adj.* unlikely to harm or upset anyone

upset - *adj.* mildly distressed

anxiety - *n.* unpleasant emotion that is experienced in anticipation of some (usually ill-defined) misfortune

threat - *n.* a warning that something unpleasant is imminent

panic - *n.* overcome by a sudden fear

bullying - *n.* act of intimidating a weaker person to make them do something

perfectionism - *n.* a disposition to feel that anything less than perfect is unacceptable

4 Are You a Confident or an Anxious Person?

Task 1: Decide whether you agree or not with the statements.
Task 2: Decide which statements would refer to a confident (C) person and which to an anxious (A) person?

1. You get attacks of *shaking* or *trembling*.
2. You rarely have *nightmares*.
3. You occasionally have thoughts and ideas that you would not like other people to know about.
4. You do not need understanding friends to *cheer you up* - you can cheer yourself up by yourself.
5. You often worry about things you should not have done or said.
6. You sometimes feel *miserable* for no good reason.
7. You sometimes gossip - it's only *harmless* fun.
8. You sometimes talk about things you know nothing about.
9. You suffer from sleeplessness.
10. You worry about awful things that might happen.
11. You are not constantly trying to please those around you.
12. You tend to think a lot about the cause of your successes and failures
13. You feel as bad when you fail a mock exam as you would if you'd failed the real one
14. Winning a debate matters more to you than making sure no one gets *upset*.

ANXIOUS

1, 3, 5, 6, 9, 10, 12, 13

CONFIDENT

2, 4, 7, 8, 11, 14

INTERPRETATION (NOT TO BE TAKEN SERIOUSLY!)

We all experience *anxiety* every once in a while. It is a normal response to a stressful event or a perceived *threat*. Anxiety can range from feeling uncomfortable and worried to serious moments of *panic*. Anxiety is an unpleasant feeling of fear or impending disaster and reflects your thoughts and reactions of your body when you are presented with an event or situation that you feel you will not be able to manage or deal with successfully. Although a minimum of concern is a normal response to a stressful situation, when its level becomes too high, we are put in difficulty, therefore losing the power to handle the stressful situation or threat. Sometimes we literally freeze, we try to avoid a situation or even react abnormally to the fear.

What causes anxiety? A number of factors can contribute to the development of anxious thoughts and behaviors. Some personality types are more at risk than others. The most shy, with low self-esteem, have higher chances of incurring the anxiety traps or styles of thought. Firstly, research has shown that some people with a family history of anxiety are more likely (though not always) to experience anxiety. Secondly, some experiences in life can make people more susceptible to anxiety. Events such as family disintegration, abuse, *bullying* at school, and conflict in the workplace can be stressors. Another factor is a tendency to *perfectionism*, if you tend to want to have a constant control over your emotions, you are more likely to develop forms of stress and anxiety.

Clearly, the more 'yes' answers you gave the 'anxious' statements, the more anxious you are.

5   Are You a Morning or an Evening Person?

Glossary

diurnal - *adj.* occurring every day

yuk - *n.* a sound/exclamation made to express disgust

continental breakfast - *n.* in British English used to specify a (simple) breakfast that is typical of Europe as opposed to the characteristic 'full English breakfast'

yummy - *adj.* extremely pleasing to the sense of taste

mellow - *adj.* relaxed, easygoing, genial

croupier - *n.* someone who works at a gaming table in a casino

casino - *n.* place for gambling and entertainment

trendy - *adj.* in accord with the latest fashion

stall-holder - *n.* someone with a vending point at a market

lounge - *n.* a sitting room in a house

navy blue - *adj* color typical used on military ships or naval uniforms

pastel - *adj.* delicate and pale in color

primrose - *n.* a yellow flower

brass band - *n.* orchestra that plays brass instruments (i.e. wind instruments that consist of a brass tube)

pour your heart out - *exp.* tell someone your deepest feelings in a prolonged spurt

lend a sympathetic ear - *exp.* listen to someone with understanding and compassion

resort - *n.* frequently visited tourist location

sun-drenched - *adj.* covered with sunlight

night owl - *n.* a person who likes to be active late at night

shun - *v.* deliberately avoid

hell - *n.* a cause of difficulty and suffering

peak - *v.* to reach the highest point; attain maximum intensity

early bird - *n.* someone who gets up very early in the morning

night shift - *n.* working period that takes place at night typically in manual jobs but also in hospitals

5   Are You a Morning or an Evening Person?

Discover your '*diurnal* dynamics' by answering these questions.

1. What is the first thing you do in the morning?

    a Check to see if you are still alive.
    b Make a cup of tea or coffee.
    c Jump out of bed and do your exercises.

2. When you are staying at a hotel, what do you order for breakfast?

    a Breakfast – *yuk*! You never touch it.
    b A *continental breakfast*.
    c All the *yummy* things you don't have time to cook at home.

3. Imagine you are going for a job interview, when do you think you would you make your best impression?

    a After a sauna and a visit to the hairdresser.
    b Just after lunch when your prospective boss is hopefully *mellow*.
    c At the first appointment of the day.

4. Providing the pay was the same, which would you apply for as a part-time job?

    a A *croupier* in a *casino*.
    b A receptionist.
    c A *trendy* market *stall-holder*.

5. When do you usually go jogging or take other forms of exercise?

    a After tea in the evening.
    b Lunchtime or afternoon.
    c Before work in the morning.

6. When you are looking for a new house or flat, in which direction do you prefer the house to face?

    a West.
    b North or south.
    c East.

7. What colors best suit a *lounge*?

    a Deep, dark dramatic tones, such as wine red or *navy blue*.
    b Practical, natural colors, such as green and brown.
    c Light and bright *pastel* shades, such as *primrose* yellow.

8. Which type of music do you prefer?

    a Cool jazz.
    b Classical symphonies.
    c *Brass band* marches.

9. If your best friend wants to *pour his/her heart out*, when should they phone you for a good reception?

   a At the end of the day when you could *lend a sympathetic ear*.
   b Anytime – that's what friends are for.
   c Before you leave for work.

10. When you fly abroad on holiday, what is your favorite view on landing?

    a The *resort* ablaze with lights.
    b Looking down on a *sun-drenched* beach.
    c A panoramic view of the rising sun.

SCORE

Give yourself 3 points for each 'a' answer, 2 points for each 'b', and 1 for each 'c'. This should give you a total score of something between 10 and 30.

25-30 POINTS

You are in the *night-owl* category, *shunning* the daylight and coming into your own after sundown. This is no problem if you work in the evenings, but it must be *hell* if you have to start work at 9.0 am. Remember that these daily cycles are fixed by habit as much as by nature, so you can, if you wish, adjust your lifestyle so as to *peak* earlier.

15-24 POINTS

You may be gratified to know that you are normal – capable of adjusting fairly easily either to a daytime or night-time existence. You know that truly restful sleep is obtained with good food, exercise and fresh air, not stimulants or sleeping pills.

10-19 POINTS

You are the original *early-bird*, which is ideal provided that you do not work a *night shift*. More likely you have discovered the secret of good living.

Chapter 2
Risks and Sensations

6 Do You Like Taking Risks?

Glossary

exotic - *adj.* characteristic of another (apparently more exciting) place or part of the world

starter - *n.* food or drink to stimulate the appetite usually served before a meal or as the first course

fruit machine - *n.* mechanical device for gambling, typically found in bars, cinemas

fun fair - *n.* amusement park

roundabouts, **carousels** - *n.* rides typically chosen by young children when at a fun fair

blast - *v.* play music at a very high volume

drawer - *n.* a box-like container in a piece of furniture

fret - *v.* worry

bonds, stocks, shares - *n.* forms of financial investment

start up - *n.* very new enterprise/company

fire practice - *n.* the act of simulating and preparing for a possible fire

fraud - *n.* deliberate dishonest behavior intended to gain an advantage

threat - *n.* a warning that something unpleasant is imminent

hazard *n.* potential danger

pollution - *n.* contamination with harmful substances as a consequence of human activities

skydiving - *n.* performing acrobatics in free fall

edge - *n.* limit

well-rehearsed - *adj.* practiced many times in order to be ready for something

6 Do You Like Taking Risks?

Task 1: Decide which of the two options you would normally follow in your own life.
Task 2: For each trio of options, decide which would be the typical risk-taker (mark these with an R) response, and which would be typically answered by someone who is very cautious (C).

1. You go to a new restaurant. Which would you choose:

   a Anything that sounds foreign and *exotic*.
   b A new *starter*, but the main dish would be something I've had before.
   c Something you recognize and know you will like.

2. You are playing on a *fruit machine* and finish all the coins you had in your pocket. Do you:

   a Change a big note convinced that you'll hit the jackpot.
   b Stop.
   c Borrow a couple of coins off a friend.

3. At a *fun fair* which rides do you like to take the most?

   a *Roundabouts* and carousels.
   b When I am strapped in, taken high up in the air, and then fall at the speed of sound to the ground.
   c A water splash.

4. You are at home playing your favorite music. Do you:

   a Have the volume as high as it will go and *blast* it out through your biggest speakers.
   b Keep it quiet - you don't want to disturb the neighbors.
   c Close all the windows and doors, and play it loud.

5. You need to find a guarantee form for a product that has just broken. You:

   a Find it immediately - it's in the *drawer* with all your other guarantees.
   b Would never find it - who keeps guarantees anyway?
   c Find it eventually, after a bit of *fretting*.

6. You win the national lottery and decide to invest a substantial part of your winnings. In what?

   a Government *bonds*.
   b *Stocks and shares*.
   c A new social media *start-up*.

7. The fire alarm goes off at work. Would you:

   a Immediately go out into the street.
   b Go into the next room and see what's going on there.
   c Carry on - it'll just be the usual *fire practice*.

8. You want to buy something on an online site you've never used before. What do you do:

   a Write down your numbers both from the front and back of the card - what's the problem? Credit card companies always refund you in the case of *fraud*.
   b Before providing your credit card details, you do a web search to see if any customers have had any problems with this retailer.
   c Pay using PayPal or some other accredited payment service provider.

9. You are about to go on holiday for a week. You have to leave in 5 minutes to be at the airport on time. However your washing machine still has 15 minutes of its cycle left. Do you:

   a Turn it off and leave for the airport.
   b Wait for it to finish its cycle.
   c Leave it on and go the airport.

10. You are in your car in a hurry to get back home to watch a football match on TV. You could save ten minutes by driving up a street the wrong way. The street is 50 m long. Do you:

    a Drive the wrong way up the one-way street.
    b Take the longer route.
    c Reverse up the one-way straight.

INTERPRETATION

In the Middle Ages the concept of risk was always associated with external causes, natural events like a storm, a flood or an epidemic, rather than to a situation deliberately created by man. Today, the term risk is generally used exclusively with reference to negative or undesirable outcomes. It thus indicates *threats*, *hazards*, dangers or damage. Technically, the term 'risk' refers to situations in which there is a decision whose consequences depend on the outcome of future events with known probabilities. However in most cases our knowledge of these probabilities is not so exact and often decisions are made in conditions of uncertainty or ignorance.

In terms of health, risk can be a danger to your health due to external factors, for example, *pollution*, industrial waste, toxic additives in food; over which we have a very limited control. Then there are risks that are the result of certain lifestyles or harmful behaviors such as smoking, poor eating habits, lack of physical exercise etc.

Research into the extreme sport of *skydiving*, found that "risk-taking" was a challenge that an individual sets him/herself in order to assess their ability to deal with a risky situation. This type of activity is defined as 'edgework' i.e. a behavior at the *edge* of what is normally acceptable, and thus a risky or radical behavior.

RISK TAKER (R)

1) a 2) a 3) b 4) a 5) b 6) c 7) c 8) a 9) b 10) a

If you have four or more risk-taker answers you are clearly running your life on the edge. You are probably a sensation seeker (see next quiz).

CAUTIOUS (C)

1) c 2) b 3) a 4) b 5) a 6) a 7) a 8) c 9) a 10) b

If you have four or more cautious answers you are living very far from the edge and feel safe only when your feet are firmly on the ground and you are following *well-rehearsed* routines. You can double check your levels of cautiousness by doing the test entitled 'How cautious are you?'

NORMAL

1) b 2) c 3) c 4) c 5) c 6) b 7) b 8) b 9) c 10) c

If you have answered with only b's and c's, then your attitude to taking risks falls within the norm.

7 Are You a Sensation Seeker?

Glossary

murder - *n.* premeditated killing of a human being by another human being

bullfight - *n.* spectacle where a matador baits and (usually) kills a bull in an arena before many spectators

argument - *n.* heated discussion (i.e. where there is strong disagreement)

prescription - *n.* written instructions from a physician or dentist to a pharmacist concerning the form and dosage of a drug

just for the hell of it - *exp.* just for fun

yearn - *v.* desire, want badly

threshold - *n.* the starting point for a new state or experience (in this specific case, level of tolerance)

7 Are You a Sensation Seeker?

Task 1: Reply 'yes' or 'no' to the statements below.
Task 2: Decide to which statements a typical sensation-seeking person would reply 'yes'.

1. I like to read newspaper accounts of *murder* and other forms of violence.
2. I would like to see a *bullfight* in Spain.
3. I like to follow instructions and to do what is expected of me.
4. I am easily bored and need plenty of excitement, stimulation and fun.
5. I would much prefer listening to hard rock and metal than classical music.
6. I can still be friendly with people who do things that I consider to be wrong.
7. I tend to act impulsively.
8. I sometimes do dangerous things *just for the hell of it*.
9. I think people should be quick to adapt to new technologies.
10. I would prefer to go on an organized tour in a foreign country than to organize my own itineraries.
11. I like to have structured well-defined tasks as an integral part of my daily routine.
12. I like to dress to catch attention.
13. I enjoy having an *argument* even if the topic is not very important.
14. I only take medicine upon *prescription* from my doctor.
15. I hate having to wait for people.
16. I don't like planning in advance - it takes away all the fun.
17. I like to be at the center of attention.
18. I would prefer to drive 10 km under a speed limit, than 10 km over a speed limit.

SENSATION SEEKER

A sensation seeker would typically answer 'yes' to the following: 1, 2, 3, 4, 5, 6, 7, 8, 12, 13, 15, 16, 17.

INTERPRETATION

SENSATION SEEKER

If you answered yes to eight or more of the 'sensation-seeking' questions. Then you match the following profile:

A sensation seeker refers to a type of personality in constant search for new and intense sensations, and who is willing to take risks to get them. If you are a sensation seeker then your prime interest is not in the risk itself, but is a consequence of the fact that the strongest feelings can be experienced, often, only in extreme situations. You have a very low tolerance to boredom and predictability. Taking drugs, jumping out of a plane with a parachute, racing in very fast cars, mountain climbing and other extreme sports are all behaviors that provide the sensations that a sensation seeker *yearns* for. But it comes at the cost of putting your own safety at risk as well as that of the people around you.

ROUTINE SEEKER

If you answered yes to less than three of the 'sensation-seeking' questions. Then you match the following profile:

You are clearly not a sensation seeker. You are not even attracted by activities of high emotional intensity but which are low-risk, such as listening to certain types of music, watching erotic or horror movies, trips to exotic countries, and parties without using drugs. Your *threshold* for boredom is much higher than a sensation seeker's. You are not always looking for the latest innovations, the latest release of intoxicating experience, or the best way to reduce the level of predictability in your life.

8 How Cautious Are You?

Glossary

gossip - *n.* light informal (but potentially malicious) conversation

gut instinct - *exp.* what your brain spontaneously tells you is the right thing to do

cast one's vote - *v.* officially express your preference for a particular candidate or option

entail - *v.* involve

wise - *adj.* having good judgment or common sense in practical matters often (but not necessarily) acquired in later life

sensible - *adj.* showing reason or sound judgment

reckless - *adj.* marked by defiant disregard for danger or consequences

8   How Cautious Are You?

1. If I have an opportunity to get into a concert without paying and be sure I am not seen, I would

    a probably do it.
    b certainly not do it.

2. If I am about make a long journey

    a I always check the overall safety (brakes, lights, oil, petrol) of my car.
    b I just check that I have enough petrol.

3. For me *gossip* is something

    a I never indulge in - you never know whether it might get back to the person you're gossiping about.
    b harmless and fun.

4. In order to get out of something that I don't want to do

    a I always explain why I don't want to it - it's always best to tell the truth.
    b I will sometimes pretend that I am ill.

5. When crossing a road with other people

    a I am normally the first to cross.
    b I look very carefully both ways before crossing.

6. When preparing for my summer holidays

    a I tend to wait till the last minute before deciding where to go.
    b I plan everything at least three months in advance.

7. Before voting in a general election

    a I thoroughly investigate the qualifications of all the candidates.
    b I use *gut instinct* on the day of the election to help me cast my vote.

8. Regarding my personal finances

    a I would never get into more debt than I could handle.
    b I have no issue with buying things on credit even if it means I might accumulate quite a bit of debt.

9. When I need some important document

    a it usually takes me a while before I can locate it.
    b I keep all my important papers in a special cabinet where I can easily locate them.

10. Locking myself out of my car and house is

    a not something I have ever experienced
    b is not unusual for me.

SCORE

Score one point for each of the following answers:

1) b 2) a 3) a 4) a 5) b 6) b 7) a) 8) a 9) b 10) a

8-10 POINTS

Caution is often associated with excessive concern about what is apparently right and wrong, and if you scored highly on this test you are focusing too much on this factor. In reality, being cautious does not mean avoiding danger or difficult decisions, or always acting in self-preservation. On the contrary, doing the right thing usually *entails* courage.

5-7 POINTS

Caution is a virtue often misunderstood and underestimated. Being cautious means making *wise* decisions based on what you see before you. If you scored between 5-7 points, then your approach is both normal and reasonable. You tend to act in a way that avoids unnecessary risks - and this is both practical and *sensible*.

2-4 POINTS

You frequently fail to demonstrate proper concern about the possible bad results of your actions. You risk getting into major trouble.

0-2 POINTS

You appear to be unconcerned about the consequences of your actions. You are very *reckless*.

9 How Spontaneous Are You?

Glossary

buzzing - *adj.* noisy like the sound of a bee

spike - *n.* sudden peak (typically found in graphs, but in this specific case used in a metaphorical sense)

prank - *n.* joke

long for - *v.* desire strongly or persistently

on the spur of the moment - *exp.*- spontaneously

charades - *n.* game in which participants act out a phrase for others to guess

dare - *n.* a challenge to do something dangerous

on the fly - *exp.* while already in progress, spontaneously

open-minded - *adj.* ready to entertain new ideas

stick to details - *v.* never deviate from the details

idealistic - *adj.* believing in some (possibly unattainable) morals, values and principles

9 How Spontaneous Are You?

Task 1: Decide whether you agree or disagree with the statements below.
Task 2: Re-read the statements and decide which ones indicate a person who tends NOT to be spontaneous in their behavior.

1. You are rarely the center of attention in a group of people.
2. Your mind is always *buzzing* with unexplored ideas and plans.
3. Your work style is a random collection of energy *spikes* rather than being methodical and organized.
4. You generally do and say things quickly without stopping to think.
5. You hate being with a crowd who play jokes on one another.
6. You like doing things in which you have to act quickly.
7. You like going out a lot.
8. You like playing *pranks* on others.
9. You would rather improvise than spend time coming up with a detailed plan.
10. You like talking to people so much that you never miss a chance of talking to a stranger.
11. You often *long for* excitement.
12. You often do things *on the spur of the moment*.
13. You prefer to have few but special friends.
14. You suddenly feel shy when you want to talk to an attractive stranger.
15. You stop and think things over before doing anything.
16. You are good at games like *charades* or doing improvisational acting.
17. You rely more on your experience than your imagination.
18. You would do almost anything for a *dare*.
19. You like buying presents for friends and family on the spot.
20. You are able to make decisions *on the fly*.

INTERPRETATION

If you answered 'yes' to questions 1, 5, 13, 14, 15 and 17, and predominantly 'no' to the other questions, then you are someone who likes to keep their feet well planted on the ground and whose head never ventures towards the clouds.

If you answered 'no' to questions 1, 5, 13, 14, 15 and 17, and predominantly 'yes' to the other questions, then you are clearly getting a lot of fun out of life. You love to be creative. You like lively and *open-minded* people. Your sense of humor, enthusiasm and energy inspire those around you. You communicate well and enjoy entertaining others.

However there are potential downsides to your personality:

- you can be too impulsive
- you tend to need constant recognition
- you do not like working alone
- you have problems with routine
- you are not great when having to *stick to details*
- you are probably a little too *idealistic*

10 What Is Your Attitude Towards Driving and Drivers?

Glossary

hitch - *v.* travel by getting a free ride from someone

convenient - *adj.* suitable

discreet - *adj.* unobtrusive

dexterity - *n.* very good at using one's hands

top of the range - *exp.* the best in its category

hurl abuse - *v.* utter a rude expression intended to offend

threaten - *v.* express an intention that is likely to go against the wishes of the person receiving the threat

adverse - *adj.* contrary to your interests

10 What Is Your Attitude Towards Driving and Drivers?

1. If your car breaks down do you

   a look in the instruction book
   b flag someone down
   c *hitch* to the nearest garage
   d call a taxi

2. You are a passenger in a car which is being driven too fast by someone you don't know very well. You begin to get nervous and frightened

   a say nothing and pray silently
   b wait for a convenient moment to start talking about accidents and bad driving
   c make discreet little signs indicating that you are frightened
   d tell him/her openly that you are scared

3. You are driving alone in your car and get stuck in a slow-moving traffic jam. How do you usually react?

   a I forget the traffic jam and stare dreamily at anything that looks interesting
   b I try not to get agitated
   c I tap the wheel in irritation
   d I get angry and hoot the horn and shout out of the window

4. You are walking down a street and see the driver of a car with one hand on a mobile phone and the other holding a cigarette.

   a You admire the driver's *dexterity*.
   b You think "Either the phone or the cigarette, but not both - that's a bit dangerous."
   c You shout abuse.
   d You shout abuse, make a note of their number plate and immediately contact the police.

5. Your best friend buys a new car - a *top of the range* Mercedes. How do you feel?

   a Very happy for your friend.
   b You can't wait to ask him/her to have a test drive.
   c You are jealous that he/she can afford such a car.
   d You focus on the fuel consumption and how environmentally-unfriendly it is to have large cars.

6. You are outside the home of someone who has been hosting a dinner party. You notice someone getting into their car. You know that he/she has had at least one bottle of wine to drink.

   a You too have had about a bottle and are easily capable of driving.
   b You hope that the person drives carefully.
   c You go up to the driver and suggest he/she comes in your car or gets a taxi.
   d You *hurl abuse* at the driver and *threaten* to call the police if they drive away.

SCORE

PREDOMINANTLY A'S

You are probably a relaxed driver, a relaxed passenger, and positive-thinking and relaxed person. However, you should probably think about taking your responsibilities more seriously.

PREDOMINANTLY B'S

You are a practical person. Whenever you are in a particular situation you generally react in a sensible way, and sometimes see an opportunity in a potentially *adverse* situation.

PREDOMINANTLY C'S

You are not particularly tolerant of cars, their owners, and the way people drive in general.

PREDOMINANTLY D'S

You have strong reactions to most situations. You believe you have a clear sense of what is right and wrong, and you do not tolerate what you consider to be bad drivers.

Chapter 3
Confidence Levels

In this chapter the glossaries of the five tests are all listed here.

11 Are You Assertive?

tip - *n.* money given for services rendered (e.g. in a restaurant or bar)

create a fuss - *v.* create a state of agitation or an angry disturbance

be trampled on - *v.* let yourself be treated with contempt

short notice - *n.* without advance notification

get away with - *v.* manage to do something without any of the foreseen negative consequences

trait - *n.* a distinguishing feature of your personal nature

bulldozing *adj.* aggressive

12 How Easily Do You Get Embarrassed?

white lie - *n.* a statement (considered of no great importance) that deviates from the truth

stare - *v.* . watch/observe in a fixed manner

flustered - *adj.* thrown into a state of agitated confusion

sympathy - *n.* understanding, affinity

struggle - *v.* find difficulty

to be kidding - *v.* joke

13 How Strong Is Your Personality?

cut off - *v.* end

horn - *n.* a noise made by the driver of an automobile to give warning

cut corners - *exp.* not complete tasks as they should be

tactfully - *adv.* showing diplomacy

pushy - *adj.* rather aggressive

submissive - *adj.* willing to submit to orders or wishes of others

14 How Confident Are You?

captivated - *adj.* filled with wonder and delight

topless beach - *noun.* a sandy area near the sea where women can relax without the top half of a bikini

overly - *adv.* to an excessive degree

demure - *adj.* affectedly modest or shy, especially in a playful or provocative way

deluded - *adj.* believing that you have a particular quality when in fact you probably don't

a turn off - *n.* something unattractive

a turn on - *n.* something attractive

15 How Much Do You Like To Be in the Spotlight?

procrastinate - *v.* postpone doing what you should be doing

rely - *v.* have confidence or faith in

drama - *n.* a highly (and probably unnecessarily) emotional episode

proffer - *v.* present for acceptance or rejection

11 Are You Assertive?

1. In a restaurant you feel the quality of the food and the service has been poor. Which of the following actions do you take?

    a. *Tip* the waiter the standard amount and complain to your friends afterwards.
    b. Decide not to leave a tip and tell the management just why you are dissatisfied.

2. A relative phones you at work when you are very busy and don't want to talk. Do you

    a. Talk with the relative and feel stressed and impatient.
    b. Tell the relative you really are too busy and don't want to talk.

3. You are in a hurry and you see a long queue at a supermarket checkout counter. Do you:

    a. Wait in the queue and get increasingly irritated about the lack of help.
    b. Insist that the manager open another checkout.

4. You feel that you deserve a promotion or a salary raise. Do you:

    a. Wait until your boss decides to do something about it.
    b. Discuss the matter urgently with your boss.

5. You are asked to make the arrangements for an office party when you would rather not. Do you:

    a. Go ahead and do it because you don't like to *create a fuss*.
    b. Say you are not interested in doing it and refuse.

6. Your boss asks you to stay late, and you have a very important personal appointment. Do you:

    a. Cancel your appointment and work late to please your boss.
    b. Tell your boss that your appointment is important and that working late at such *short notice* is impossible.

7. You are about to speak, and someone interrupts you. Do you:

    a. Let it pass and allow the other person to speak for you.
    b. Announce that you have just been interrupted, and that you'd prefer to speak for yourself.

SCORE

MOSTLY A'S

You tend to let people *get away with* things and have it their own way rather than insisting on your own rights. If you answered a) to all seven questions then you are risking having your life *trampled on*. You need to adopt some strategies typically used by assertive people. First you need to set boundaries as to what you consider is and is not acceptable. If someone crosses that 'acceptability line' then you should intervene. Secondly, you need to command the respect of those around you. Speak up, let yourself be heard when someone appears to be totally disregarding your needs.

MOSTLY B'S

While putting your needs first may be a healthy *trait* some of the time, if you answered b) to most of the questions, you are not merely being assertive but instead have a *bulldozing* approach. You need to aim to be somewhere in between. Being assertive is about respecting both yourself and the other person but without compromising the other person's rights as a human being. While you should aim to build strong relationships with others, you also need to hear (and try to understand) what others have to say even if you do not necessarily agree with them.

12 How Easily Do You Get Embarrassed?

Look at the following situations and decide whether you would find the situation embarrassing or not. Answer 'yes' or 'no'.

1. Someone tells a joke that I don't understand.
2. I spill a drink over the carpet at someone's house.
3. I arrive at a party wearing the wrong type of clothes.
4. Someone asks me a personal question that I would prefer not to answer.
5. I am in class and want to ask the teacher a question.
6. I forget my partner's birthday.
7. I don't like the food that your host has just put in front of me.
8. I break something in a shop.
9. The meal I have just eaten in a restaurant was very poor. I feel the need to complain to the manager.
10. Two people in the corner of the room are clearly talking about me,
11. Someone makes a nice compliment about the way I look.
12. My partner starts shouting at me in the street.
13. I have to give a presentation to a group of 10 people.
14. Out with friends, I realise I don't have enough money to pay for the meal we've just had.
15. Someone has posted a ridiculous photo of me on Facebook.
16. I am caught out telling a *white lie*.
17. I arrive late for an appointment with people I don't know.
18. I get lost in my car and my passenger is someone who I am trying to impress.
19. I say something that is immediately proved wrong by someone else present.
20. I lose my temper with a friend.

SCORE

Give yourself one point for every 'yes' answer.

15-20 POINTS

You are constantly feeling that people are *staring* at you and judging you - your face is burning, you're feeling all *flustered*, and in the worst possible scenarios you even feel immobilized. You need to remember that showing embarrassment is not necessarily a negative thing. It acts as a kind of apology to those around you - they can see the physical signs on your face that you are 'sorry' for what you have done. So in cases such as 2, 3, 8 and 18, you will actually elicit the *sympathy* of those around you. However, if you get embarrassed so often and so easily, you may need to work out in your head why it is that you feel such constant embarrassment. You need to work on your confidence.

10-14 POINTS

Your level of embarrassment is within the norm. And in fact it may actually be working in your favor - your red face is merely a sign that you care about other people, and your open expression of this embarrassment is nothing harmful as it will actually make people like you more. However, if you are *struggling* to deal with it, you need to work on ways on raising your levels of self confidence.

5-9 POINTS

You need to be careful because your clear level of self confidence may seem to others like arrogance.

0-4 POINTS

Who are you *kidding*? You have either completely lost touch with the world around you or are living a life of total delusion. What's so bad about a bit of embarrassment every now and then?

13 How Strong Is Your Personality?

1. I find it difficult to say 'no' to the demands that other people make on me.
2. If someone jumps the queue and passes in front of me, I tell them to go back.
3. I usually put myself second in family matters.
4. If I receive poor service at a restaurant, I tell the manager.
5. I find it hard to leave a situation even when I have had enough.
6. In a meeting, of whatever kind, I like to take command.
7. I would never hesitate to ask a stranger in the street for help.
8. I believe that we should always fight for our rights - if we don't, we are in danger of losing them.
9. I don't have any issue with in quickly *cutting off* an unsolicited call with a salesperson.
10. I frequently use my *horn* when driving.
11. If someone is talking too much I find it difficult to find an excuse to leave.
12. I am happy to get ahead even if this means *cutting corners* here and there.
13. I tend to tell people what they want to hear if this will further my aims.
14. When going out for dinner with a group of friends, I tend to be the one who chooses where we are going to go.
15. I tend to dominate most conversations - both social and at work.

SCORE

If you answered predominantly 'yes' to questions 2, 4, 6-10, and 12-15, you have what others may *tactfully* call a strong personality. You insist on other people respecting your rights, and may even be seen as *pushy*. Your behavior may be bordering on aggression - be careful, don't try to deprive others of their legitimate rights.

If you answered 'yes' to questions 1, 3, 5 and 11, and 'no' to the majority of the other questions, you are *submissive*, a follower rather than a leader, and easily taken advantage of.

14 How Confident Are You?

1. You are standing in a lift with someone you don't know.

   a. You avoid all eye contact.
   b. You ask them what floor they are going to.
   c. You tell them a one-line joke that you've just read in a magazine.

2. A TV company is doing a street interview about the political elections about to take place.

   a. You cross the road as soon you see the TV crew.
   b. You agree to be interviewed, but fail to express yourself well.
   c. You deliver a perfect speech and consider going into politics yourself.

3. You are at a job interview.

   a. You speak very quietly.
   b. You hide your nerves by speaking slowly and loud.
   c. You look the interviewers in the eyes and speak clearly.

4. You are making conversation with someone at a party. The person listening to you is

   a. Getting more and more bored the longer you talk.
   b. Probably interested in what you are saying.
   c. *Captivated* by every word you say.

5. You find yourself on a *topless beach*. You think

   a. I'll just go near the dunes where no one can see me.
   b. OK, this is cool by me.
   c. This is absolutely the best way to sunbathe.

6. You walk into a room at a party and everyone seems to turn around and stare at you.

   a. You become very anxious assuming that everyone thinks that you are wearing something that they wouldn't seen dead in.
   b. You ask the person with you to explain what's going on.
   c. This is usual for you. You turn heads wherever you go.

7. You would be happy to receive a compliment from someone who said:

   a. What a great job you're doing holding down a job and bringing up a family.
   b. Well done on the job promotion.
   c. You are looking particularly sexy today.

MOSTLY A'S

You are rather shy and perhaps *overly* modest.

MOSTLY B'S

You have found the right balance between being too *demure* and being over confident.

MOSTLY C'S

You have an extremely high (and possibly rather *deluded*) opinion of other people's opinion of you, imagining that everyone who looks at you will find you immediately amazing. For many people such arrogant behavior will certainly be *a turn off* ... however a few may find it a massive *turn on*.

15 How Much Do You Like To Be in the Spotlight?

Part 1

For each sentence decide which part (a or b) that is most similar to you.

1. Do you believe that it is more rewarding to be

    a) liked by others b) powerful?

2. Do you consider yourself more

    a) practical b) creative?

3. Do you enjoy going to social events where

    a) people partake in intellectual discussions b) there is heavy alcohol consumption?

4. In stressful situations, do you

    a) generally feel anxious b) manage to remain calm?

5. Do you have a tendency to

    a) *procrastinate* b) get things done immediately?

6. As a general rule, do you

    a) let other people influence your actions b) make all your own decisions?

7. Do you prefer being

    a) on the margins b) at the center of attention?

8. Is feeling relaxed when talking in front of many people

    a) difficult for you b) easy?

9. Do you

    a) worry too much about what other people think b) simply not care?

10. At a party do you prefer to

    a) sit down and watch the others b) dance the night away?

Part 2

Now decide which of these characteristics match your personality and which don't.

11. You tend to think before speaking, thereby reducing your chances of hurting or misunderstanding those around you.
12. You have good listening skills. You silence allows you to open your ears and be truly attentive.
13. You have a good understanding of other people as you tend to enjoy observing human behavior in social settings.
14. You are quite independent and resourceful. You have learned to *rely* on yourself rather than on others.
15. You like to dress in a way that makes you appear very attractive.
16. Your friends tend to know all about you, what you've done, what you did, what you are doing and what you plan to do .... because you are always keeping them informed.
17. You like/need to create a *drama* every now and then.
18. You tend to be both compulsive and impulsive.
19. As a child you felt the need to attract your parent's attention away from other things and on to you.
20. In a conversation at a dinner party, you like to direct the discussion and constantly *proffer* your opinions.

SCORE

Shyer people tend to choose the (a) answers in the first part, and statements 11-14 in Part 2.

Attention seekers tend to choose the (b) answers in the first part, and statements 15-20 in Part 2.

Chapter 4
Trust, Honesty, Altruism and Ambition

16 How Trusting and Trustworthy Are You?

Glossary

check up on - *v.* investigate, verify

keep something back - *v.* refrain from mentioning

Airbnb - *n.* online marketplace and homestay network enabling people to list or rent short-term accommodation in residential properties

crowdfunding - *n.* practice of funding a project or venture by raising monetary contributions from a large number of people

decline - *v.* refuse politely

stand - *v.* how you feel about, what your position is in relation to something

beneath - *adv.* under

go blind - *v.* enter a situation with your eyes closed, i.e. without really thinking about what you are doing

consistency - *n.* always following the same logic and behavior

humility - *n.* the opposite of arrogance

16 How Trusting and Trustworthy Are You?

PART 1

1. If someone suggests a wonderful place to go on holiday, do you?

   a *check up on* it
   b *take them up on* their idea
   c stick to your original plans

2. Do you pick up hitchhikers?

   a never
   b quite often
   c depends what sex they are

3. If someone knocks at your door, do you?

   a open it immediately
   b with the door shut ask who it is
   c open the door with the chain attached

4. When you make a new friend do you

   a confide your personal life immediately
   b get them to talk as much as possible
   c only tell them your secrets when you really know them well

5. On holiday where do you keep your money

   a in your back pocket
   b in a bag around your neck
   c in the hotel safe

6. When you vote do you generally?

   a ask someone's advice beforehand
   b rely on your intuition
   c read various newspapers and then come to a decision

7. How much of a newspaper do you generally believe?

   a 95%
   b 75%
   c 50%

8. You are thinking about earning some money by renting your home out on *Airbnb*. To what extent would you trust potential guests to leave your home exactly as they found it?

   a 95%
   b 75%
   c 50%

9. You are thinking about investing some money through *crowdfunding*. What do you think are the chances of you seeing your money again?

   a 95%
   b 75%
   c 50%

10. Someone offers to take you home in their car after a party where vast quantities of alcohol have been consumed. He/she claims that they haven't drunk 'much'. Do you?

    a Have no problem accepting the lift.
    b Ask them to drive carefully.
    c Politely *decline* the offer.

PART 2

Now decide if you match the following characteristics. You are able to:

- admit it when you do not know something
- be both flexible and reliable
- disagree without needing to argue
- keep agreements or renegotiate if necessary
- let others know how you feel, and where you *stand* in relation to them
- make compromises but not in relation to core principles or personal integrity
- recognize, accept, and enjoy the differences between you and your colleagues/family

> **SCORE**
>
> PART 1
>
> This part investigates how trusting you are of others.
>
> MOSTLY A'S
>
> You are so trusting of others that sooner or later you are going to get a nasty shock. Try to look a bit *beneath* the surface, and start questioning people's motives.
>
> MOSTLY B'S
>
> You don't *go blind* into situations, however you have probably had a few negative experiences as a result of trusting someone too much.
>
> MOSTLY C'S
>
> Most of the time you are fully aware of whether you can trust someone or not. In any case, you are adverse to taking risks.
>
> PART 2
>
> This part looks at the extent to which you inspire trust in others.
>
> If you answered 'yes' to the majority of the questions, then you will probably have most (if not all) the following characteristics: authenticity, compassion, *consistency*, *humility*, integrity, kindliness, supportiveness.

17   How Honest Are You?

Glossary

wardrobe - *n.* piece of furniture that provides storage space for clothes

slot machine - *n.* a machine for gambling typical found in bars, cinemas etc.

root of all evil - *exp.* the prime cause of everything that is bad

gambling - *n.* the act of playing for stakes (money) in the hope of winning

chess - *n.* an ancient board game for two players who move their 16 pieces according to specific rules

risk your shirt - *v.* undertake a venture without regard to possible loss or injury

addictive - *adj.* making you unable to stop (typically of a bad habit)

17   How Honest Are You?

1. You find a wallet in the street full of dollars and credit cards. The owner is obviously very rich and their address is in the wallet.

    a You pocket the money and throw the wallet away.
    b You pocket the money and send the wallet to the owner.
    c You contact the owner and arrange to send the entire contents to him/her.

2. You are working in a foreign country. You discover you can earn a lot of money without paying tax.

    a You take the money and don't pay the tax.
    b You pay the tax like an honest citizen.
    c You report your boss to the authorities for trying to give you black market money.

3. You rent some new rooms. In a *wardrobe* in one of the rooms you find a fully functional money printing machine.

    a You immediately start printing money.
    b You leave the machine where it is.
    c You inform the police.

4. You are on holiday abroad and discover that you can use coins from your own country in the local *slot machines*. The equivalent coin in your host country is worth five times as much as your coins.

    a You don't use your coins.
    b You use your coins.
    c You use the coins, and next time you return you take a large supply of extra coins.

5. You are given change for a $50 note in a supermarket. You in fact only gave them a $20 note.

    a You tell the assistant
    b You say nothing
    c You say nothing and go again next day hoping the situation will be repeated.

6. You are in a jeweler's shop and no one else is around. On the counter is a diamond ring; nobody would know if you took it. What would you do

    a I'd be very tempted but wouldn't take it
    b I'd actually take it
    c Nothing. Temptation is not a word in my vocab

7. Which of the following do you believe in?

   a money is a necessary evil
   b the love of money is the *root of all evil*
   c money *breeds* money
   d money is power

8. What are your views of *gambling* as a form of entertainment?

   a not much, you prefer games like *chess* where luck doesn't play a part
   b you find the idea of *risking your shirt* attractive but in practice pull out quickly if you don't win
   c you find the excitement of being in the hands of fate totally *addictive*
   d you like the chance element but prefer those kinds where mathematical probability or experience give you some control

SCORE

A strong tendency towards dishonesty: 1 a, 2 a, 3 a, 4 c, 5 c, 6 b, 7 d, 8 c

Completely honest to the point of righteousness: 1 c, 2 c, 3 c, 4 a, 5 a, 6 c, 7 b, 8 a

Like most people: a mix of answers - tempted by some situations but overall honest.

18 How Altruistic Are You?

Glossary

struggle - *v.* have great difficulty

water - *v.* salivate

tease - *v.* ridicule, harass, provoke

taunting - *v.* abuse vocally by deriding, mocking or criticizing

sticks and stones may break my bones but words will never hurt me - *exp.* your violence might affect me physically, but nothing that you say to me will injure me

bedraggled - *adj.* in a very bad condition

flag someone down - *v.* stand at a roadside attempting to stop a passing car in order to be helped

guilty - *adj.* feel unease because you did something bad to someone or did not do something that you should have done

charity flag day - *n.* an activity to raise money for an institution set up to provide help to the needy

jangle - *v.* shake a metallic container (in this case a money collection tin) in order to attract attention

run - *v.* manage

thoroughly - *adv.* completely

selfish - *adj.* concerned only with yourself to the exclusion of others

do your bit - *exp.* make your contribution

fool yourself - *v.* give yourself the wrong impression

sainthood - *n.* the status of a saint, i.e. a person acknowledged as holy or virtuous in the Christian faith

18 How Altruistic Are You?

1. You see an old lady *struggling* to cross the street with some heavy bags.

    a You ignore her, she should get herself a shopper's trolley.
    b You help her to cross.
    c You help her to cross and then offer to carry her bags home for her, even though she lives in the opposite direction.

2. At a dinner party there's one more chocolate left in the bowl.

    a You take it and eat it when no one's looking.
    b You offer it to the others first.
    c You insist that someone else have it, though your mouth is *watering*.

3. You run over a cat in your car.

    a You carry on driving.
    b You stop and knock at the presumed owner's door.
    c After calming down the owner you offer to take the cat to the vet.

4. A neighbor's car alarm goes off in the middle of the night.

    a You close the window and put your ear plugs in.
    b You ring the neighbor but do nothing more if there's no reply.
    c You rush round to investigate.

5. You see some children *teasing* and *taunting* another child.

    a Based on the old saying that *Sticks and stones may break my bones but words will never hurt me,* you do nothing.
    b You warn the children, but do nothing more if they persist after you've left.
    c You break up the group and threaten to inform their parents.

6. You are driving along a country road in the dead of night. A *bedraggled* person of unknown sex tries to *flag you down*.

    a It's probably some drunken maniac.
    b You drive past and feel terribly *guilty* that you didn't stop.
    c You stop immediately and give whatever assistance is needed.

7. It's some *charity flag day* and they're *jangling* money boxes on the street.

    a You cross over to the other side of the street.
    b You reluctantly donate 50c.
    c You happily put a $20 note into the collection box.

8. You see a young teenager stealing sweets from the corner shop *run* by an old couple.

   a You remember when you used to do the same.
   b You tell the teenager that you've seen what they did.
   c You inform the shopkeepers.

> **SCORE**
>
> MOSTLY A'S
>
> Some might say that you are *thoroughly selfish*. Perhaps you need to start thinking about others rather than just yourself.
>
> MOSTLY B'S
>
> You *do your bit* to help the world, albeit rather half-heartedly.
>
> MOSTLY C'S
>
> The world would certainly be a better place if everyone was like you. A sarcastic interpretation would be that either you're *fooling yourself*, or that you'll shortly be in line for *sainthood*.

19 How Nice Are You?

Glossary

practice what you preach - *exp.* act in accordance with how you say that you should act

foul - *adj.* unpleasant

be better off - *exp.* be in a better position/situation

put yourself in someone else's shoes - *exp.* project yourself into someone else's predicament and understand how they feel

bear a grudge - *exp.* maintain resentment or anger against someone for a past offense

keep your cool - *exp.* maintain your calm in a difficult situation

19 How Nice Are You?

1. No matter who I am talking to, I'm always a good listener.
2. I am happy to admit it when I make a mistake.
3. I try to *practice what I preach*.
4. When I don't know something, I have no problem in admitting it.
5. Even if someone is *foul* to me, I will still try to be agreeable.
6. I have never deliberately said something that hurt someone's feelings.
7. I believe that if you give the average person a job to do, he/she will finish it successfully.
8. People usually tell the truth even when they know they would *be better off* lying.
9. Attempts to understand ourselves are a waste of time.
10. If you are popular as a child you will be popular as an adult too.

If you answered 'yes' to the majority of questions 1-8, most people are likely to consider you to be a nice, sincere and decent person. So what areas do you need to work on if you want to be a nice (nicer) person? Typically the following adjectives are used to describe 'nice' people:

- considerate - someone who takes other people's feelings into consideration before saying something or taking a particular course of action
- empathetic - someone who is able to *put themselves in someone else's shoes* and relate to their situation
- forgiving - someone who doesn't *bear grudges* and understands that it is only human to make errors
- fun - someone who has a sense of humor and can see the funny side of a situation
- modest - someone who is able to be humble and does not take themselves too seriously
- patient - someone who *keeps their cool* in the face of difficulty
- self-aware - someone who is conscious of their own behavior and limits, and has a sense of self criticism
- strong - someone who is mentally strong and resilient to push forwards

20   How Tactful Are You?

Glossary

pensioner - *n.* someone who is no longer in employment and who receives money (a pension) from the state

to be starring - *v.* to be the most important performer or have the most important role

play - *n.* a theatrical performance

proud - *adj.* feeling good about yourself or someone close (partner, member of family, colleague) due to your/their very good performance

dreadful - *adj.* exceptionally bad or displeasing

hideous - *adj.* extremely ugly

to be short of - *exp.* to have an insufficient amount of something

cheap and cheerful - *exp.* despite not being expensive, an object or place that is sufficiently pleasant

upset - *v.* cause an emotional disturbance

20 How Tactful Are You?

1. Your friend has just come out of the hairdresser's. You say:

   a I know a lawyer who can help you to sue whoever cut your hair like that.
   b It looks a bit short, but hey it'll soon grow again.
   c Hey, I like your new look.

2. You see a *pensioner* inadvertently put something in their pocket instead of the trolley. You would:

   a Report them to manager.
   b Go up to them and point out what they have done.
   c Do nothing.

3. At a dinner party the hosts have served inedible food. You would:

   a Let everyone know how awful the food is.
   b Eat a few mouthfuls and then push the plate to the side.
   c Try and eat everything you can.

4. You go to watch a school play *starring* the child of your good friend who is sitting next to you. The *play* is really bad. You say:

   a Sorry, but I really am going to have to leave in the interval.
   b I see that school plays haven't got any better since we were at school together.
   c Your kid is so great, you must be so proud.

5. You receive a *dreadful* birthday present from an old aunt and uncle. You would:

   a Tell them you think it is *hideous*, and ask whether it was actually a joke on their part.
   b Say nothing, and open the next present.
   c Thank them, take it home but never use it.

6. You are planning to go to a restaurant with a group of friends, one of whom is *short* of money at the moment. Would you suggest going to

   a Your usual restaurant which is really rather expensive.
   b A medium-priced restaurant which at least all the others can afford.
   c A *cheap and cheerful* restaurant, where the food is still good.

7. A friend has just had a baby - rather ugly - which you are now seeing for the first time. You say:

   a Oh dear, what happened to you!
   b She has a very interesting face.
   c What a lovely smile and a lovely girl.

8. You are just leaving a supermarket and another customer drops all their bags in front of you. Would you

   a Laugh heartily and leave.
   b Pretend you haven't noticed.
   c Help them collect their shopping.

SCORE

MOSTLY A'S

You have clearly never heard of the concept of being 'diplomatic'. The fact that you tell people exactly what you think may be appreciated by some people on some particular occasions, but most of time you are probably going around *upsetting* people.

MOSTLY B'S

You know how to be tactful but sometimes you lose your patience and tell people around you what you think.

MOSTLY C'S

You hate upsetting the balance. You wish to maintain calm at all times. As a consequence you tend to be positive, considerate and helpful. However, be careful your tactfulness may at times be interpreted as insincerity.

21 How Ambitious Are You?

accomplish - *v.* gain with effort

take something to heart - *exp.* take criticism seriously and be affected or upset by it

civil service - *n.* public administration, government work

equate - *v.* be equivalent, similar, equal, or analogous to something else

destroy - *v.* damage irreparably

lifespan - *n.* the period between birth and death

21 How Ambitious Are You?

Read the sentences carefully and answer with true (T), false (F), or partly true (PT). There are no right or wrong answers in this test, since what matters most is your opinion. Try to answer as spontaneously as possible. If any of the questions do not directly apply to you, try to imagine yourself in the situation.

1. I am annoyed when people who are not more intelligent than me achieve more.
2. I am not a good loser.
3. I consider people who *accomplish* nothing to be less valuable to society.
4. I could not become very enthusiastic about any activity that gets little recognition.
5. I enjoy party games because I always try to win.
6. I find solving difficult problems stimulating.
7. I like to compare my achievements with those of other people.
8. I *take criticism very much to heart.*
9. I try to develop my weaker qualities through training.
10. I will watch television programs and videos on YouTube, even though I may find them uninteresting, if I think I can profit from them.

11. I would have liked to have been top of the class at school.
12. I would like to do better than my parents.
13. I would prefer a fairly insecure job with good promotion prospects to a quiet and secure job in the *civil service*.
14. It is very important to me that others appreciate my achievements.
15. My professional career is more important to me than many other things.

> **SCORE**
>
> The more T answers you have given, the more ambitious you are.
>
> If you answered T to more than 10 questions you need to be aware of the potential dangers of being overambitious. One problem is that as children we are often taught that ambition is a key determiner for success. But it really depends on what you define as 'success'. Research has frequently found that money and status don't necessarily *equate* with happiness or even with satisfaction. In fact, ambition is only weakly connected with well-being and may actually *destroy* your relationships with others and even lead to a shorter than average *lifespan*.

Chapter 5
Health and Body

In this chapter the glossaries are all listed together below.

22   How Healthy Are You?

flights (of stairs) *n.* section of a staircase between one floor and another

breathless - *adj.* able to breathe only with difficulty

fill someone with delight - *exp.* provide a feeling of extreme pleasure or satisfaction

defy - *v.* go against

count - *v.* rely on

23   How Happy Are You With Yourself?

bitter - *adj.* marked by strong resentment or cynicism

resentful - *adj.* full of resentment and ill will

trait - *n.* typical characteristic

face up to - *exp.* address a problem and try to deal with it

deny - *v.* declare untrue

comfort zone - *n.* a situation where you feel safe and at ease

24 How Happy Are You With Your Body?

resigned - *adj.* having come to accept

overly - *adv.* to an excessive degree

self esteem - *n.* an attitude of admiration, approval and liking of and for oneself

comfortable - *adj.* free from stress, accepting

wellbeing - *n.* a contented state of being happy, healthy and prosperous

25 How Obsessed Are You About Your Job?

overtime - *n.* work done in addition to regular working hours

workaholic - *n.* person with a compulsive need to work

26 Are You a Victim of Stress?

mistake someone for someone else - *exp.* think that someone is another person

teasing - *n.* playful provocation

in a rush - *exp.* needing to do something quickly, under pressure to do something

burden - *n.* load, weight

22　How Healthy Are You?

Which questions, if answered 'yes', would indicate that you are probably living a healthy life?

1. At any point during the last week have you walked more than 2 kilometers on a single walk?
2. If you have to go up more than two *flights*, do you usually take the lift?
3. Do you try to limit your intake of sugary, fatty or salty food?
4. Do you usually grill food rather than fry it?
5. On most days, do you eat at least two portions of fresh fruit?
6. In the space of a week, do you drink 14 or fewer units of alcohol?
7. Do your gums sometimes bleed when you brush your teeth?
8. Are you *breathless* if you have to walk up four flights of stairs?
9. Do you often fall asleep when it is not actually bedtime?
10. Do you often take work home with you?
11. Is your blood pressure less than 120 over 80?
12. If you are over 30, has your weight changed increased more than 3 kg in the last five years?
13. When possible, do you tend to eat organic food?
14. Does the idea of big fat steak *fill you with delight*?
15. Do you use semi-skimmed milk rather than full-fat milk?
16. Do you catch colds more often than most other people you know?
17. Do you have your cholesterol levels checked regularly?

SCORE

Healthy lifestyle: 1, 3, 4, 5, 6, 11, 13, 15, 17

If you answered yes to most of the 'healthy lifestyle" answers then you are already taking the most of the right steps for health and fitness. However, if you answered no to many of the 'healthy' answers, you have *defied* medical theory ... so don't *count on* it lasting forever.

23 How Happy Are You With Yourself?

1. Do you ever wish that you looked like someone else who you judge to be physically attractive?
2. Do you always want to know how others have performed on a test that you have just taken?
3. Do you use words like 'normal' and 'average' to describe yourself?
4. Are you always looking to make friends on Facebook?
5. Do you get upset if only a few people 'like' something you have posted on Facebook?
6. Do you find yourself having to announce your *accomplishments* to others?
7. Do you get upset when you can't get your point across to other people?
8. Do you spend a lot of time analysing by yourself the relationships that you have with friends and colleagues?
9. In a classroom do you always sit at the back?
10. Do you look back at family holidays with a sense of sadness?

> SCORE
>
> If you answered 'yes' to six or more of the questions then most people would define you as being 'unhappy'. Typical *traits* of unhappy people include an inability to:
>
> - enjoy the good fortune of others, instead you tend to be rather *bitter* and *resentful*
> - *face up to* various issues in your life and to resolve them. You have a tendency to *deny* that you have a problem that probably most of those around you are aware exists
> - help others
> - make true friends
> - move out of your *comfort zone* - you refuse to take any risks, and as a consequence your situation remains static with no hope of improvement
> - take responsibility for your life, instead you tend to blame other people or general circumstances for your difficulty
> - view the positive aspects of life

24 How Happy Are You With Your Body?

Look at the parts of the body and body attributes below. For each part decide how satisfied you are on a scale of:

- A - not happy at all, embarrassed
- B - *resigned*
- C - reasonably happy
- D - very satisfied, very fortunate

bottom	facial complexion	nose
build	fingers	profile
chest	hair	shape of head
chin	hands	teeth
distribution of hair over body	knees	voice
ear	legs	weight
eyes	neck	width of shoulders

Score

mostly As

You are *overly* critical of yourself about your appearance. This could have a negative impact on your *self esteem*. Learn to be more accepting of yourself. No one is perfect.

a mix of Bs and Cs

You are often too influenced by the way your culture and society interpret the physical impression that someone makes. It is highly likely that you are unrealistic both about how you body really looks and how you think it should look. Try to ensure that you have a more emotionally healthy and a positive sense of *self*.

mostly Ds

You are *comfortable* with the way you appear to yourself and the way you appear to others. Your confidence and *wellbeing* are benefitting from this attitude.

25 How Obsessed Are You About Your Job?

Answer 'yes' or 'no' to the following questions.
1. I am hoping to be promoted within the next six months.
2. I would like to be given roles with more and more responsibility.
3. I'd rather make the wrong decision than waver too long to make the right decision.
4. I will try to avoid *overtime* - not only does it take up too much time, but I also believe it is a kind of exploitation.
5. Other people's criticism doesn't bother me.
6. I find it difficult to enjoy a holiday because I would rather be at work.
7. The most important things that happen to me involve work.
8. I am always trying to think of ways of doing my job more effectively.
9. It makes me unhappy when my work is not up to its usual standard.
10. I can do my boss's job better than he/she can.
11. I am happy to tell my boss if I think he/she has done something wrong.
12. I tend to take my job responsibilities more seriously than my personal and family responsibilities.
13. When at home I find it difficult to relax and clear my mind of work-related matters.
14. I feel I am able to influence the decisions taken by my immediate supervisor.
15. I spend most weekends working.

SCORE

If you answered 'yes' to questions 6, 7, 8, 9, 12, 13 and 15 you are a *workaholic*. You spend far too much time either being at work or thinking about work. You should consider shifting some of your priorities to other aspects of your life (family and leisure).

If you answered with a mix of 'yes' and 'no' you have a healthy attitude to work.

26 Are You a Victim of Stress?

Part 1

1 At the airport in a foreign country some officials stop you after you have just gone through passport control.

   a No problem - they must have *mistaken* you for someone else.
   b You are sure that you will miss your flight.

2 Your boss has just asked you to make a mini presentation in a meeting which is due to begin in 10 minutes.

   a You feel nervous.
   b You are calm and confident.

3 Heavy traffic blocks you on the way to a meeting.

   a You immediately use your mobile to inform your colleagues.
   b You do nothing and apologize when you arrive.

4 Your superiors are carefully monitoring a project you are working on.

   a You are happy that they are taking an active interest in your work.
   b You're worried that they might find something seriously wrong with your work.

5 You have been invited to an interview. The secretary says: "Ms Jones will see you in a minute." An hour has now passed.

   a You feel angry and frustrated.
   b You feel relaxed and sure that an excellent new job is just round the corner.

6 At a project meeting yesterday some of your colleagues teased you about some of your ideas.

   a You still feel quite angry and embarrassed.
   b A bit of *teasing* never harmed anyone.

Part 2
Answer yes or no to the following questions.

 1 Are you very competitive?
 2 Do you often take work home with you or study for long hours at a time?
 3 Do you have to travel a lot for work or study?
 4 Do you get very nervous before examinations (both academic and medical)?
 5 Are you always *in a rush*?
 6 Are you a good listener?
 7 Do you often get angry with the stupidities of other drivers?
 8 Are you worried about what people think of you?
 9 Are you patient when waiting in queues?
10 Do you normally show your feelings?

SCORE

PART 1

You are totally stressed out if you agreed with the majority of the following questions:

1 b, 2 a, 3 a, 4 b, 5 a, 6 a

You are a very relaxed and positive person if you agreed with the majority of the following questions:

1 a, 2 b, 3 b, 4 a, 5 b, 6 b

PART 2

If you answered *yes* to six or more of questions 1-5 and 7-8 and *no* to the others, you are leading a very stressful life and you should take active steps to reduce your stress *burden*.

If you answered *yes* to three or four of these questions, you are rather too worried much of the time and perhaps too ambitious.

If you answered *yes* to two of the questions, your level of stress indicates that you lead a normal relaxed life.

If you answered *no* to the above questions and *yes* to 6 and 9, then you are incredibly relaxed - you are almost asleep!

Chapter 6
Image, Imagination and Communication

27 How Important Are Personal Image and Ambition for You?

Answer each sentence with 'true' (T), 'false' (F) or 'partly true' (PT).

1. I would have liked to have been top of the class at school.
2. I believe that if I don't pay attention to my personal image at work I will stand less chance of being promoted.
3. If I had the choice I would prefer a fairly insecure job with good promotion prospects to a quiet and secure job in the civil service.
4. It annoys me if people who are not more intelligent than me achieve more.
5. If I had more money I would buy more status symbols such as a self-drive car, the latest iPhone, a personal robot.
6. If someone criticizes me, I am affected and upset by it.
7. If I am going to a meeting or presentation I make sure I wear very smart clothes.
8. If I hadn't worked so hard earlier in my life, I wouldn't be where I am today.
9. If I can I would like to do better than my parents.
10. I never think about what I more I could have done in a particular situation, I simply focus on what I can do now.

> **SCORE**
>
> Give yourself two points for every 'true', one point for every 'partly true'. No points are scored for 'false' answers. Add up your points for the 10 questions.
>
> 17-20
>
> Very strong: Your personal image and sense of ambition tend to rule over your life.
>
> 14-16
>
> Strong
>
> 11-13
>
> Average to strong
>
> 8-10
>
> Average to weak
>
> 0-7
>
> Weak: Your personal image and sense of ambition have little importance for you in terms of how you lead your life.

28 How Imaginative Are You?

Glossary

parcel - *n.* a package that has been wrapped

fancy dress party - *n.* party where people wear costumes

extra-terrestrial - *n.* a creature from another planet

recipe - *n.* directions for making something in the kitchen

fairy godmother - *n.* someone imaginary who helps you when you are in a difficult situation

pet - *n.* domestic animal (cat, dog, rabbit) typically treated like a member of the family

take something to the next level - *exp.* progress to a higher and better point/stage

gift - *n.* a present

fairly - *adv.* to a moderately sufficient extent or degree

wonder - *n.* the positive feeling aroused by something strange, surprising or wonderful

boundary - *n.* a limit past which people should not cross

think outside the box - *exp.* not to think in the usual standard way, but instead think laterally in order generate unusual approaches or solutions

28 How Imaginative Are You?

You have 60 seconds to complete this quiz. Answer each question. If you can't think of an answer move on to the next question.

1. A mystery *parcel* arrives for you from another country. What does it contain?
2. You have the opportunity to choose any job you wish. Which job?
3. You're invited to a *fancy dress party*. What would you go as?
4. You've formed a pop group. What would you call it?
5. You're an inventor. What machine or device would you invent?
6. You meet an *extra-terrestrial*. What does he/she/it look like?
7. Someone rings you up a three in the morning. Who is it?
8. You've invented a new *recipe*. What are three of the ingredients?
9. You meet your *fairy godmothe*r. What do you ask her for?
10. You choose a new *pet* for your household. What animal or bird is it?

SCORE

Give yourself 1 point for every question you managed to answer. This should give you a total score of something between 1 and 10

9-10 POINTS

You have taken you imagination to *the next level*. Some of the greatest scientists and brains of the last millennium - Leonardo da Vinci, Isaac Newton and Albert Einstein - had a strong imagination like yours.

7-8 POINTS

You have an extremely developed sense of the imagination. You use this wonderful *gift* to keep you ahead of the game.

4-6 POINTS

Your life is *fairly* routine. You don't come up with quick solutions and go through life without necessarily experiencing the beauty and *wonder* around you.

1-3 POINTS

You appear to have little or no imagination. You create *boundaries* around yourself, and the concept of *thinking outside the box* is totally alien to you.

29 How Do You Communicate?

Glossary

tell someone off - *v.* reprimand

keep something back - *v.* refrain from mentioning

burp - *v.* expel wind noisily from the stomach through the mouth

gossip - *v.* speak about others behind their back and reveal secrets or intimacies

pet - *n.* domestic animal (cat, dog, rabbit) typically treated like a member of the family

digestible - *adj.* capable of being digested (i.e. understood)

non-verbal cues *n.* indicators of what someone is feeling revealed through their body language rather than what they are saying

straightforward - *adj.* direct, free from ambiguity

29 How Do You Communicate?

1. Which is the most difficult for you:

    a showing someone affection?
    b *telling someone off*?
    c complaining about bad service?
    d remembering what you want to say?

2. Do you understand communication better by:

    a body language?
    b the written word?
    c voice?
    d actions and behavior?

3. When you make a new friend do you:

    a confide your personal life immediately?
    b get them to talk as much as possible?
    c tell them your secrets when you know them well?
    d always *keep something back*?

4. Do you feel more embarrassed when:

    a You don't understand a joke?
    b When you say something you shouldn't have?
    c You have to undress at the doctor's?
    d You *burp* at a restaurant?

5 Who do you touch and accept being touched by:

   a Colleagues and acquaintances?
   b Close friends?
   c Members of family and partner?
   d Partner only?

6 Which do you dislike most:

   a being *gossiped* about?
   b being the center of attention?
   c people referring to you as 'normal'?
   d people referring to you as 'strange'?

7 If you could have only <u>one</u> of the following in your house which would you have?

   a books and magazines
   b computer
   c music
   d a *pet animal*

8 When round a dinner table with friends or colleagues, do you tend to:

   a dominate the conversation
   b encourage the others to talk
   c listen or talk where appropriate
   d say nothing all evening

9 When you make a phone call do you try to

   a make yourself understood
   b say what you want to say as quickly as possible
   c remember what it is you've got to say
   d listen only to the other person

10 Do you understand people who communicate better by

   a body language
   b the written word
   c voice
   d action and behavior

> SCORE
>
> There are no right or wrong answers. However, good communicators tend to have the following traits in common: They:
>
> - Are always willing and quick to help.
> - Are good listeners.
> - Ask pertinent questions that show they are following and understanding what is being said.
> - Easily relate to others (i.e. try to understand those that they are communicating with).
> - Focus exclusively on the communication without being distracted (e.g. don't check their phone while talking to you).
> - Keep everything simple by clarifying and making their message easily *digestible* by others.
> - Recognize *non-verbal cues*.
> - Use *straightforward* unambiguous language, never try to be smart just for the sake of it.

30 How Strong Are Your Psychic Powers?

Glossary

out-of-body experience - *n.* apparently supernatural state where you feel that you have left your body

trance - *n.* a psychological state as if induced by a magical incantation

séance - *n.* a meeting at which people attempt to make contact with the dead

ghost - *n.* supernatural appearance of a dead person

haunted - *adj.* apparently inhabited by a ghost

reincarnation - *n.* doctrine/belief that person may be reborn

moronic - *adj.* ridiculous

harness - *v.* control; keep in check

inner self - *n.* your personal, internal identity

figment of the imagination - *n.* a contrived or fantastic idea

30 How Strong Are Your Psychic Powers?

Answer 'yes' or 'no' to the following questions.

1. Have you ever had an *out of body experience* or unconsciously entered a *trance* state?
2. Have you ever sent thoughts to other people and had proof that they received them, or vice versa?
3. Have you heard a 'voice' calling your name - yet there is no source?
4. Have you ever successfully participated in a serious *séance*?
5. Have you ever really seen a *ghost* or felt the effects of being in a *haunted* place?
6. Have you ever experienced something moving apparently without normal cause?
7. Have you ever been successively hypnotised?
8. Do you find yourself finishing a sentence for someone because you intuitively know what is going to be said (rather than making a logical assumption about what they're going to say)?
9. Do you believe in *reincarnation*?
10. Have you 'sensed' or 'felt' strong impressions not shared by others present?

Decide whether the score on the next page was:

a) written to be taken seriously, particularly by people who believe that they may have psychic powers
b) intended to be tongue in cheek, i.e. to make fun of people who believe in supernatural powers

SCORE

Give yourself one point for every 'yes' answer.

9-10 POINTS

Excellent - you are probably communicating better with the dead than the living. You should consider helping your local police force in solving crimes. Or even better, offer your services to your government.

7-8 POINTS

Very good - you should give serious thought to deeper development of your psychic potential. Find people (friendly ghosts?) to help you.

4-6 POINTS

To you the concept of psychic powers is not entirely clear - is it mythical, magical or *moronic*? Despite this, even a score of 4 indicates that you would still be able to *harness* the psychic powers that until now have remained hidden in your *inner self*.

1-3 POINTS

Your psychic powers are seriously underdeveloped. If you are interested in really getting in touch with your spirit, then you need to realise that developing your psychic side can enrich your life.

0 POINTS

You're living in the real world and know that extra sensory perception, ghosts, and out of body experiences are merely a *figment of the imagination*.

31   To What Extent Do You Live in Your Own Dream World?

Glossary

intriguing - *adj.* capable of arousing interest or curiosity

sheer - *adj.* complete and without restriction

introspective - *adj.* given to examining your sensory and perceptual experiences

intuitive - *adj.* obtained through intuition rather than from reasoning or observation

selfless - *adj.* concerned for the welfare of others rather than your own needs

loyal - *adj.* showing constant support for a person

gentle - *adj.* having or showing a kindly or tender nature

aid - *v.* help

disposition - *n.* your usual mood

sensitive - *adj.* being susceptible to attitudes, feelings, or circumstances

31 To What Extent Do You Live in Your Own Dream World?

Answer yes or no to the following questions.

1. Do you often contemplate the reasons for human existence?
2. Do you often feel as if you have to justify yourself to other people?
3. Do you often find yourself lost in thought when you are walking in nature?
4. Do you often spend time exploring unrealistic yet *intriguing* ideas?
5. Do you rarely do something just out of *sheer* curiosity?
6. Do you rarely get carried away by fantasies and ideas?
7. Do you see yourself as very emotionally stable?
8. Would you call yourself a dreamer?
9. Do your dreams tend to focus on the real world and its events?
10. Do your emotions control you more than you control them?

Now decide which of the following adjectives apply to your personality:

Abstract	Future-focused	Private
Adaptable	Idealistic	*Selfless*
Artistic	Imaginative	Values-oriented
Caring	Independent	Warm
Creative	Internally aware	
Easygoing	*Introspective*	
Empathetic	*Intuitive*	

SCORE

If you ticked most of the adjectives and answered 'yes' to questions 1, 2, 3, 4, 8 and 10, and predominantly 'no' to the other questions, then you are dreamer. You probably have a *loyal* and *gentle* nature, *aided* by your idealism and sensitive *disposition*. Your social media pages are probably dominated by the causes you believe in, which are likely to include helping others, searching for world peace. You are driven by emotion and can thus act quite randomly and spontaneously. You dislike conflict, are very *sensitive* and easily hurt.

Chapter 7
Friends' Family and Partners

In this chapter all the glossaries are listed together below.

32 What Kind of a Friend Are You?

juicy - *adj.* suggestive of sexual impropriety

stuff - *n.* unspecified belongings

hideous - *adj.* extremely ugly

lie - *v.* not tell the truth

33 What Do You Look For in a Partner?

to be matched - *v.* be suited

domestic chores - *n.* cleaning and tidying activities around the house

34 How Well Does Your Partner Know You and Do You Know Your Partner?

compatible - *adj.* able to exist and perform in harmonious or agreeable combination

curse word - *n.* offensive word used to express anger or annoyance

ticklish spot - *n.* location on your body that is susceptible to being tickled (i.e. light touching by another person of one of the parts of your body in a way that is slightly irritating but makes you want to laugh)

to mind - *v.* be concerned and bothered with or about something or somebody

bargain - *n.* an advantageous purchase

thrill rides at a fun fair - *n.* activities causing high levels of sensation at an amusement park

fair amount - *exp.* adequate; considerable quantity

35 How Well Do Your Family Know You?

pointless - *adj.* serving no useful purpose

tidy - *adj.* marked by good order and cleanliness in appearance or habits

guilty - *adj.* feeling responsible for something that you have done (or not done)

36 What Kind of a Parent Are You (Would You Be)?

hang on to - *v.* keep

upbringing - *n.* experience acquired during a person's formative years

once in a blue moon - *exp.* extremely rarely

obey - *v.* do what someone tells you to do

32 What Kind of a Friend Are You?

This test should be done in conjunction with the next test: "What do you look for in a partner?"

Look at the following situations. Choose the answer that you think is what a really good friend would do or choose. There are no correct answers' and hence no score. Instead you should compare your answers with your close friends. If they have similar answers to you' then you are perfectly matched as friends. If they don't have similar answers' then you clearly have different expectations of each other.

1 You know a *juicy* story about your friend.

   a I tell everyone I know.
   b I tell people but without revealing the person in question.
   c I keep it to myself.

2 You just saw a very good friend's partner kissing someone else.

   a I immediately tell my friend.
   b I later ask the friend's partner what they were doing or why they did it.
   c It's none of my business.

3 My definition of a true friend is someone who:

   a Tells me everything.
   b Tells me just what I want need to know.
   c Keeps their thoughts to themselves.

4 Your friend accidentally drops your phone and the screen cracks.

   a I say I needed a new one anyway.
   b I ask them to pay for it.
   c I don't let them pay for it but tell them that they need to be more careful.

5 Your friend is always borrowing your *stuff* but never gives it back. Now they want to borrow something that has a strong emotional attachment for you.

   a I lend it to them.
   b I say I no longer have the thing that they want.
   c I politely refuse.

6 Your friend has just bought a *hideous* shirt.

   a I say nothing and start talking about something else.
   b I *lie* and say that I like it.
   c I tell the truth.

7 An ideal friend should be:

   a As intelligent as me if not more so.
   b Less intelligent and less talented than me.
   c About the same as me.

33 What Do You Look For in a Partner?

Rate the following in terms of how important they are for you in terms of your ideal partner.

3 = essential

0 = not important at all

There is no score to this test. Instead you could try comparing your answers with those of your partner. If they have similar answers to you' then you are perfectly *matched*. If the majority of your answers are different' then you clearly have different expectations of each other and should thus think hard about whether you really are suited to each other.

- a desire to have children
- a desire to have a home of your own
- ability to communicate
- acceptance of them exactly as they are
- equal capacity to respond to each other's emotional needs
- equal sharing of *household chores*
- financial security
- good relationships with each other's parents
- shared sense of humor
- similar cultural and educational background
- similar hygiene standards
- similar intelligence
- similar interests
- similar religious and political views
- similar social class
- similar views on punctuality

34 How Well Does Your Partner Know You and Do You Know Your Partner?

The next two tests you can do with your partner. You can do them in three ways.

- Either: Do the test separately and write down the answers both for yourself and for your partner. For example' for question 1 you write down i) where you were born' ii) where he/she was born.
- Or: Do the test together orally. Simply make a note of when you or your partner got the correct answer. Put a cross if you or your partner put the wrong answer.
- Or. Just have fun answering the questions together' without bothering to keep a score.

If you decide to score your results' then you can do it on the basis of two factors:

i) Which of you knows the other better. In this case keep a note of all the times when only one of you gets the correct answer. Score one point for each such answer. Clearly the 'winner' is the person who gets the most points.
ii) How *compatible* you are as a couple. In this case' keep a note of those times when in answer to the same question' you both got the correct answer.

Part 1

1. In what town was he/she born?
2. What is his/her mother's maiden name?
3. How tall is he/she?
4. How much does he/she weigh?
5. What shoe size he/she?
6. What was he/she wearing yesterday?
7. What is the last item of clothing he/she takes off before going to bed?
8. What part of his/her body is he/she least happy with?
9. What part of your body does he/she like the most?
10. What personality trait does he/she most like in you?
11. What does he/she most dislike about you?
12. What is the name of his/her first boy/girl friend?
13. Which of your close friends does he/she like the least?
14. What is the first thing he/she usually does after waking up?
15. What food' if any' is he/she allergic too?
16. How many sugars' if any' does he/she take in her tea/coffee?
17. If you go out for a drink' what will he/she order for him/herself?
18. What is his/her favorite *curse word*?
19. Approximately how many friends does he/she have on Facebook?
20. Where is his/her most *ticklish spot*?
21. What is his/her favorite movie?
22. If he/she could replace you with a film star' who would it be?
23. What is the strongest fear he/she has?
24. Who is his/her favorite politician?
25. Who did he/she vote for in the last election?

Part 2

Would your partner answer 'yes' or 'no' to the following statements regarding you?

1. I always try to practice what I preach.
2. I am always willing to admit it when I make a mistake.
3. I don't like being touched by someone I don't know.
4. At times I pretend to know more than I really do.
5. I don't *mind* talking about my private life.
6. I always finish what I start.
7. I sometimes have to stop myself from talking too much.
8. I am good at keeping secrets.
9. I am loyal to my friends.
10. I'd like to live for a year in another country.
11. I think I spend too much of my time on social media.
12. I remember seeing the sea for the first time.
13. I tend to try and do too many things at the same time.
14. I prefer discovering things by myself rather than someone teaching me how to do them.
15. When shopping' I always look for a *bargain*.
16. I tend to collect useless objects.
17. I like moving things around in my room and seeing how they look.
18. It typically takes me more than 20 minutes to get ready to go to a party.
19. At a restaurant I tend not to order things I've never tried before.
20. I like *thrill rides* at the *fun fair*.

SCORE

PART 1

0- 8: You must be very confused about each other and are clearly not compatible.

9-15: You know a *fair amount* about each other but still have a lot to learn before you will be in complete harmony.

16-20: You've clearly been together for some time and have an excellent understanding.

21-25: Wow!

PART 2

There is no score for this part of the test.

35 How Well Do Your Family Know You?

In this test you have two tasks:

i) answer the questions for yourself.
ii) for each answer you give' ask a member of your family if he/she would also have answered the question in the same way as you regarding your behavior. For example' if you say that you 'lock up the house carefully before going to bed'' your family member should say whether this is true or not.

1. I lock up the house carefully before going to bed.
2. I spend too much time working in order to be able to afford *pointless* material objects.
3. I tend not to lose sleep over my problems.
4. As a child I was more afraid of the dark than most children.
5. I am a *tidy* person.
6. I am embarrassed to tell people who I work for.
7. I am satisfied with life.
8. I don't enjoy competitive games.
9. I find it difficult to take time off work without feeling *guilty*.
10. I get nervous if I have to wait.
11. I just laugh at most of the stupid things that politicians do.
12. I tend to *hang on to* all my clothes even if they don't fit me anymore.
13. I think I am contributing to the world and leading a useful life.
14. I think it is important to safeguard your future through insurance policies and pension schemes.
15. I would feel uncomfortable if dressed inappropriately at a particular event.
16. It is not easy being me.
17. I am fascinated by fire.
18. I am not keen on speaking in public.
19. People often disappoint me.
20. I always tried to get the best marks as I could at school.

SCORE

There is no score for this test.

36 What Kind of a Parent Are You (Would You Be)?

There are no correct answers to the test. Much will depend on the culture you have' your background and the kind of *upbringing* you received from your parents. The test is simply designed to get you to think about your role as a parent. You could do the test together with your partner to see if you have similar ideas.

Part 1

Choose the most appropriate answer with regard either to how you actually are as a parent (i.e. you already have children)' or how you think a parent should be (i.e. if you don't have any children).

1 How regularly do you tell your child that you care about and love him/her?

   a) every day
   b) every week
   c) every month
   d) hardly ever

2 How much time do you set aside for listening to your child's needs and complaints?

   a) none
   b) a few minutes every day
   c) a few minutes every week
   d) a few minutes every month

3 How often do you take your child to the cinema or to see some sports event?

   a) once a week
   b) once a month
   c) once a year
   d) *once in a blue moon*

4 Do you keep your child informed of what the family's plans are for the future?

   a) yes' nearly always
   b) no' not usually

5 How often do you argue with your child?

   a) all the time
   b) once a day
   c) once a week
   d) infrequently

6 If you mistreat your child in any way or make some mistake' do you always say you're sorry?

   a) nearly always
   b) generally
   c) not usually

Part 2

Decide which statements you agree with.

1. A child should always precede a request with 'please'.
2. A child should be free to choose their own friends.
3. A parent should give a child as many choices as possible.
4. A parent should restrict a child who is imposing themself on another adult.
5. A small child should be allowed to choose their own clothes and shoes.
6. A young child should always be given more than one chance to *obey* their parents.
7. Adults should arbitrate all quarrels between children.
8. If a young child's needs go against those of an adult' the child's should be given priority.
9. In the case of a disciplinary issue' a child should always be given the opportunity to explain their point of view.
10. Whenever a parent places some restriction on a child' the reason for the restriction should be clearly explained.

SCORE

There is no score for this test.

Chapter 8
Logic and Reasoning

37 Are You a Logical Thinker?

Glossary

therefore - *adv.* as a consequence

border - *n.* boundary between two nations

survivor - *n.* someone who does not die in an accident

bury - *v.* place a dead person in a grave

vegan - *n.* someone who eats no animal or dairy products at all

riddle - *n.* a question or statement intentionally phrased so as to require ingenuity in ascertaining its answer or meaning

hard wired - *adj.* genetically determined

rely on *v.* count on, exploit

intuition - *n.* instinctively knowing something without the use of rational processes

underlying - *adj.* being or involving basic facts or principles

impeded - *adj.* made difficult or slow

set something aside - *v.* put to one side and ignore for the moment

conscious reasoning - *n.* thinking that is coherent and logical

37 Are You a Logical Thinker?

Read the statements in the first line of each question. Assume that these statements are true. Then mark the conclusion that is the most logical. If in some cases two conclusions are equally logical, mark them both. If none of the conclusions are logical, don't mark any of them.

1 Dogs are animals. All animals have legs. *Therefore*:
   a) Dogs have legs.
   b) All dogs have legs.
   c) My neighbor has a dog. Her dog must have legs.

2 My secretary is not old enough to vote. My secretary has long blonde hair. Therefore:
   a) My secretary is a girl under the age of 18.
   b) My secretary is under the legal age for voting.

3 Good musicians play classical music. To be a good musician involves an incredible amount of practice. Therefore:
   a) Classical music requires more practice than jazz.
   b) Classical music requires at least as much practice as jazz.
   c) Good musicians listen to more classical than jazz music.

4 A plane crashes on the *border* between two countries (A and B). Therefore:
   a) The *survivors* should be *buried* directly on the border.
   b) The survivors should be taken back to their country of origin and buried there.
   c) The survivors should not be buried.

5 You are in your car. There is a man crossing the road in front of you. If you stop suddenly, a bus behind you will crash into the back of your car. If you don't stop, you may kill the man crossing the road. Therefore:
   a) You are driving too fast.
   b) The bus is driving too fast.
   c) You will either be hit by the bus or you will hit the man.

6 My teacher is a *vegan* and loves animals. Therefore:
   a) My teacher does not eat meat.
   b) My teacher does not eat meat and is a member of the World Wildlife Fund (WWF).

Now decide which of the following affirmations are logical.

7 Chris is very well informed - he watches the news every night.
8 Martha gets up early every morning, therefore she is not lazy.
9 Celine's feet are so long that she has to put her jeans on over her head.
10 Anna claims to have seen an iceberg that had completely melted.

ANSWERS

1) a 2) b 3) none are logical 4) survivors are living people, therefore none of the answers are correct 5) c 6) a 7-10) all illogical

SCORE

This test was a mixture of real logic testing and silly *riddles*. Give yourself one point for each question you answered correctly.

10 POINTS

If you got all six answers correct Your brain is clearly *hard wired* to do tests of logical thinking.

8 POINTS

Rather than *relying* on *intuition*, you rely on facts and data. The result is that you can see the real issue *underlying* a question on logic.

5-7 POINTS

You were probably reasonably good at good algebra and word problems at school, but you were never the top of the class.

3-4 POINTS

Your decision-making process is rather *impeded* by emotional impulses. You need to *set these aside* and just concentrate on the facts.

1-2 POINTS

You are completely lacking in the sequential logical process required to solve puzzles, even very simple ones. You are clearly relying far too much on your opinions and intuitions.

0 POINTS

Your life is ruled by intuitive thinking, but you cannot go through life without applying any kind of *conscious reasoning*.

38 Do You Think With Your Right Brain or Left Brain?

Glossary

jump to conclusions - *exp.* decide something very quickly without reasoning about it

get by - *v.* manage, succeed

gut reaction - *n.* immediate reaction not based on reasoning

deja vu - *n.* a feeling of having been somewhere or done something before

be supposed to - *v.* be (mistakenly) believed; commonly put forth or accepted as true on inconclusive grounds

critical thinking - *n.* the process of using your mind to consider something carefully

discredited - *adj.* no longer accepted; brought into disrepute

38 Do You Think With Your Right Brain or Left Brain?

Decide whether you agree with the following statements.

1. I am very proficient at making plans.
2. I sometimes *jump to conclusions*.
3. I like to put things in a sequence or order.
4. I like to daydream. I have vivid dreams at night.
5. I am logical and normally see the motivation behind people's behavior.
6. I like the creative arts.
7. I can just about *get b*y in several languages.
8. I don't have a good conception of time.
9. I have no problem in describing my feelings.
10. I often trust my *gut reaction* to situations rather than looking for hard evidence.
11. I am objective in my opinions. I try to get the facts straight before making any decisions.
12. I cry quite easily and my feelings are often hurt.
13. I am very patient and stick to a problem. I try various approaches before I get to the solution.
14. I am a romantic.
15. I really like puzzles and word games
16. I quite often experience a sense of *deja vu*.

SCORE

MOSTLY ODD NUMBERS (1, 3, 5 ETC)

You tend to think with your left brain. This means that you *are supposed to* have superior skills in *critical thinking*, language, logic, numbers, and reasoning.

MOSTLY EVEN NUMBERS (2, 4, 6 ETC)

You tend to think with your right brain, which is supposed to be best at expressive and creative tasks. This means that you tend to be creative, intuitive and able to express your emotions. You are supposedly good at recognizing faces, playing musical instruments, and using color and images effectively.

Note: The left brain/right brain theory was originally proposed in the late 1970s but has since been somewhat *discredited*. Nevertheless it is a fun way to distinguish between different ways of thinking.

39 How Versatile Are You?

Glossary

impromptu - *adj.* with little or no preparation

play sick - *exp.* pretend to be ill in order not to have to do something that you don't want to do

anecdote - *n.* short account of an incident

dull - *adj.* lacking in liveliness or interest

let yourself go - *v.* allow yourself to lose your inhibitions

obnoxious - *adj.* causing disapproval or protest

turn your hand at something - *exp.* be able to conduct a manual task or a job

jack of all trades - *n.* someone who can conduct any kind of (manual) job

struggle - *v.* find something difficult

cope - *v.* come to terms or deal successfully with

stuck - *adj.* caught; fixed

39 How Versatile Are You?

Decide whether you are or are not able to do the following.

1. Make *impromptu* speeches even on topics about which you have almost no information.
2. Argue for ideas that you don't actually believe in.
3. *Play sick* to get out of something.
4. Work for long periods of time without getting any feedback.
5. Tell a joke or *anecdote* and get all the details right.
6. Inject some life into a *dull* party.
7. *Let yourself go* and enjoy yourself a lot at a lively party.
8. Get along with loud-mouthed *obnoxious* people.
9. Play cards or board games.
10. Work to deadlines.
11. Take personal risks just for a laugh.
12. Clearly state your preference for something.
13. Break rules or violate convention.
14. Concentrate on research for an essay or project work.
15. Do two things at once, e.g. reading while listening to the news.
16. Imitate other people's voices, accents, ways of walking etc.
17. Impress or entertain others.
18. Relate to other people's feelings.
19. Change your mind.
20. Play in any position in a team sport.

SCORE

16-20 points: You can *turn your hand to* anything, *a jack of all trades*.

10-15 points: You are willing and able to adapt your behavior, and this increases your ability to communicate. You have confidence, tolerance, empathy, positiveness and respect for others.

6-10 points: You *struggle* to find opportunities and are not particularly interested in learning about new approaches.

0-5 points: You find it extremely difficult to *cope with* changes in circumstances and to think about problems and tasks in novel, creative ways. You are very much *stuck* in the way you are.

40 How Responsible Are Your Decisions?

Glossary

slot machine - *n.* a machine that is used for gambling

reimburse - *v.* pay back for some expense incurred

charity - *n.* an institution set up to provide help to the needy

beggar - *n.* a person who lives by asking people in the street for money or food

lobster - *n.* a large marine crustacean which is a culinary delicacy

teller - *n.* an employee of a bank who receives and pays out money

40 How Responsible Are Your Decisions?

Decide whether the statements below are true (T) or false (F).

1. You put a coin in a *slot machine*. You play the game, lose (so you think) all your money, and then the coin is returned to you. Rather than keep this money, you should *reimburse* the slot machine company.
2. It is better to give to an organized *charity* than to a *beggar*, even though the charity devotes half of all donations to payment of its own expenses.
3. A horse with a broken leg should be shot, for although curing the leg is possible, it is a long expensive process, and hard on the horse – unless, of course, anesthetics and pain-killers are used.
4. Baked *lobsters* should not be ordered in a restaurant because the lobsters go into the oven alive.
5. Highway *billboards* contribute much to the national business income. Nevertheless, they should be banned, because they mar the natural beauty of the countryside.
6. If you have time, better to *haggle* with a *tradesman* than to let him overcharge you.
7. You know that waiters depend on *tips* for a living. In a strange town, you go into a restaurant and get very bad service. Nevertheless, you should be tolerant enough to leave your usual tip instead of reducing it.
8. Leaving a bank, you discover that the *teller* has given you ten dollars too much. The bank and staff are insured against losses. In such a case, you might as well keep the money, since you did not steal it and it would deprive nobody.

KEY

1F, 2T, 3T, 4F, 5F, 6T, 7F, 8F

SCORE

Give yourself 2 points for each incorrectly answered question, and 1 point for each unanswered question. Add these points for your total score.

0-2

Superior (top 5% of population):

3-7

Good (next 15%)

8-13

Fair (next 30%)

14-16

Poor (lowest 50%):

41   How Well Do You Handle Your Finances?

Glossary

go into the red - *exp.* go under the permitted amount on your bank account

ruin - *n.* an irrecoverable state of destruction

outgoings - *n.* the opposite of income, i.e. money you spend on bills, household items etc.

gamble - *v.* play games for money; take a risk in the hope of a favorable outcome

41   How Well Do You Handle Your Finances?
Decide which statements indicate someone who is handling their finances well (W) and badly (B).

1. I have no idea how much money I have in my current account.
2. I tend to *go into the red* by the end of the month.
3. My bank does not charge me for my financial transactions.
4. I have three or more credit store cards.
5. I pay off the full amount of my credit card every month.
6. If I received an unexpected tax bill for $2500 I would be able to pay it.
7. If I were run over by a bus and had to spend the next six months in hospital, this would lead to my financial *ruin*.
8. If my house and everything it in it was destroyed during a fire, although it might be an emotional disaster it would not affect my finances.
9. I have no clear idea of what my monthly *outgoings* are (e.g. utilities bills, credit card payments, standing orders, travel expenses).
10. I never *gamble*.

SCORE

Well: 3, 5, 6, 8, 10

Badly: 1, 2, 4, 7, 9

Chapter 9
Work

In this chapter all the glossaries are listed together below.

42 What Kind of Job Would You Like?

plumber - *n.* person who installs and repairs water pipes

firefighter - *n.* a member of a fire department who tries to extinguish fires

enlisted soldier - *n.* man or woman who serves in an army

lumberjack - *n.* a person who cuts down trees

human resources manager - *n.* someone in charge of a group of team of people that recruits, interviews, and trains employees as well as dealing with their individual issues

surgeon - *n.* a physician who specializes in surgery, i.e. cutting open the human body to perform a medical intervention

midwife - *n.* a woman skilled in aiding the delivery of babies

broadcaster - *noun* someone who transmits a program or some information on the radio or television

butcher - *n.* a person who slaughters meat for market; someone who sells meat from a shop

oil rig - *n.* a structure with equipment for drilling an oil well; an oil platform

sewer - *n.* a waste pipe that carries away sewage or surface water

charity - *n.* a non-profit organization set up to provide help to the needy

43 What Do You Want From a Job?

autonomy - *n.* independence

prestige - *n.* a high standing achieved through success

give credit when credit is due - *exp.* recognize an achievement when it deserves praise

44 What Kind of Job Would You Prefer?

on the spur of the moment - *exp.*- spontaneously

commission - *n.* fee for services rendered based on a percentage of an amount received or collected or agreed to be paid (as distinguished from a salary)

hence - *adv.* as a result

45 You and Your Job

get on well with - *v.* have a good relationship with

advice - *n.* a proposal for an appropriate course of action

retire - *v.* stop working because you have reached a certain age

46 Should You Change Job?

company profile - *n.* sketch/analysis representing the extent to which a company exhibits various characteristics

take time off - *exp.* stop going to work for a limited period

resolution - *n.* plan to take a particular course of action

fulfilled - *adj.* satisfied

42 What Kind of Job Would You Like?

This test will help your understand your attitude towards certain professions. There are no correct answers, and hence there is no score.

1) The following jobs have been rated as 'boring' by many people but are all relatively well paid. Which of them do you think in reality would not be so boring?

   a) accountant
   b) database administrator
   c) *plumber*
   d) technical writer
   e) insurance sales agent

2) Which of the following do you think would be the most stressful?

   a) air traffic controller
   b) simultaneous interpreter
   c) top sports player
   d) newpaper reporter
   e) inner-city high school teacher

3) Which job would be the most dangerous?

   a) *firefighter*
   b) taxi driver
   c) *enlisted* soldier
   d) *lumberjack*
   e) president of the USA

4) Which do you think would be the most rewarding?

   a) *human resources manager*
   b) speech-language pathologist
   c) CEO
   d) social worker
   e) teacher

5) Which jobs do you think contribute most to society and get paid well at the same time?

   a) *surgeon*
   b) police officer
   c) *midwife*
   d) veterinarian
   e) deputy fire chief

6) Which job would be the most exciting?

   a) photojournalist
   b) *broadcaster*
   c) cook
   d) model
   e) actor

7) Which would be the most unpleasant?

   a) *butcher*
   b) waiter/waitress
   c) *oil rig* worker
   d) fisherman
   e) *sewer* inspector

8) Which would be your ideal job?

   a) lawyer
   b) engineer
   c) university professor
   d) doctor
   e) *charity* worker

43 What Do You Want From a Job?

This test is designed for recent graduates to help them evaluate what they expect from the world of work. Answer 'yes' or 'no' to the following questions.

I would like a job that ...

1. Provides opportunities to use the knowledge I gained at university and from my previous experiences.
2. Guarantees that I will have a good level of personal *autonomy*.
3. Provides me with varied tasks.
4. Will give me a stable secure future.
5. Leaves me relatively free of supervision by others.
6. Permits me to help other people.
7. Gives me the possibility to exercise leadership.
8. Allows me to grow within the company.
9. Provides plenty of opportunities for travel.
10. Offers me the opportunity to manage others.
11. Gives me the time to have fun with colleagues.
12. Lets me exploit my competitive streak.
13. Helps me to improve my skills.
14. Enables me to conduct research.
15. Gives me the opportunity to earn a lot of money.
16. Allows me to be creative.
17. Ensures *prestige* and social status.
18. Enables me to work with people not just things.
19. Ensures that I am *given credit when credit is due*.
20. Gives me a chance to see the results of my work being put into practice.

SCORE

There is no score for this test.

44 What Kind of Job Would You Prefer?

Look at the options below and decide which you would prefer: the first (F) or the second (S).

1. Always eating familiar foods OR frequently trying strange foods.
2. Climbing a mountain for pleasure OR trying to save someone.
3. Compiling a short dictionary for financial reward OR writing a short story for fun.
4. Eating special things because they are good for your health OR because you enjoy them.
5. Going to an art gallery to learn about the exhibits OR just look at the exhibits.
6. Going to evening class to improve your qualification OR for fun.
7. (At work) Having your tasks set for you OR choosing your own activities.
8. Leisure activities that have a purpose OR which are just exciting.
9. Planning a holiday OR going on holiday.
10. Planning your leisure OR doing things *on the spur of the moment*.
11. Reading for information OR for fun.
12. Recounting an incident accurately OR exaggerating it for effect.
13. Ensuring that money gets saved well OR gets spent well.
14. Spending most of the time in just one place OR spending your life in many different places.
15. Staying in one job OR having many changes of job.
16. Taking holidays principally in the same places OR in many different places.
17. Winning a game easily OR playing a closely-fought game.
18. Work that earns promotion OR that you enjoy doing.
19. Working in the garden OR picking wild fruit in a wood.
20. Working to a fixed salary on a fixed contract OR on *commission*.

SCORE

MAINLY F'S

Basically you are looking for a job that gives you security. You want to be able to go home at night knowing that you will receive your salary at the end of the month, a bonus at the end of the year, and a pension at the end of your career.

MAINLY S'S

You are driven by excitement and quickly get bored if a job (or anything else in your life) becomes too routine.

45 You and Your Job

The following questions are designed to get you to think about whether you:

- are happy with your job
- have suitable qualities to carry out your job
- could contribute more to your team and your company in general
- should perhaps think about changing jobs

Due to the exploratory nature of the questions, there are no correct answers, and *hence* no score.

1. What are the main responsibilities of your job?
2. Who are you responsible to and who are you responsible for?
3. Who do you *get on best with* at work?
4. How has your job changed over the last few years?
5. What areas of your job have been going well recently?
6. What three things do you like most about your job and why?
7. What factors affect your performance?
8. How can your performance be measured?
9. Have you ever done any training courses? If not, what kind of courses do you think would be useful for you?
10. What do you think are your best talents at work?
11. What skills do you have that are not being used in your job?
12. What *advice* would you give your boss?
13. What advice do you think your boss would give to you?
14. If you could change three things about your job, what would you change?
15. If you had not decided to follow this particular career, what path would you have followed instead?
16. How would you like to see your working relationships change or develop over the next few years?
17. Will you still be working in the same job in five years' time?
18. How do you see your future with your company?
19. What career aspirations do you have?
20. When you *retire* or leave your present company, what do you hope you will have achieved?

46 Should You Change Job?

1 It is Sunday evening – how are you feeling?

   a I am feeling very excited about the week ahead.
   b I usually don't think about work at all until I'm there.
   c I am already starting to get depressed about returning to work.

2 Your boss is going to be out of town for a few days, which of the following will you do?

   a Relax and spend time chatting to friends on the phone.
   b Take a longer than usual lunch break.
   c Carry on with your work, your boss's absence makes no difference to you.

3 What are your chances of promotion?

   a Actually they're promoting me tomorrow.
   b I am sure I'm going to be promoted within the next two years.
   c I'll probably never be promoted.

4 You are talking to someone at a party and they ask you what you do.

   a I'll give them a brief *company profile*.
   b I'll tell them my job title and tell them what projects I am currently doing.
   c I'll immediately try to change the subject.

5 Someone tells you that your boss wants to speak to you.

   a Excellent. This will be an opportunity to discuss new ideas for future projects.
   b It will probably be about something fairly routine
   c I feel panicky and nervous.

6 Where are you thinking of going on holiday this year?

   a Holidays – who needs them? I'll probably *take a few weekends off* when I can.
   b I'm going to have my usual two weeks in the summer and at the end of the year.
   c I am dreaming about my next holiday as I do this quiz.

7 What *resolutions* are you going to make for the coming months?

   a I'm going to try to improve my efficiency and productivity.
   b I'm going to carry on as I am now.
   c I'm going to look for another job.

SCORE

Score 3 points for any answer a, 2 for b and 1 for c

15 - 21

You are very optimistic and confident about both your work now and your future. You're *fulfilled*, contented and efficient but definitely not normal, however your family and friends might remark that need to forget work a little and start to enjoy the rest of your life.

8 -14

Your job's OK but it's not the most important thing to you. Very healthy!

7 - 14

You need to fill in some job applications today and get out of there as fast as possible!

Chapter 10
Effectiveness in Work Environment

In this chapter all the glossaries are listed together below.

47   Do You Have Effective Meeting Skills?

scenario - *n.* situation.

whisper - *v.* speak softly without vibration of the vocal cords

48   Are You a Good Negotiator?

pocket money - *n.* money given to a child, generally on a weekly basis

household chores - *n.* cleaning and tidying activities around the house

would rather - *v.* would prefer

top job - *n.* very good job in high position

put up with something - *v.* cope with or manage some kind of adverse situation, without actually trying to change it

fixed rate deal - *n.* amount of a charge or payment that is established at the beginning of a job to be done and which binds the party providing the service

quote - *n.* estimate of cost

trample over someone - *v.* let another person do whatever he/she wants even though this goes totally against your own best interests

49 How Well Do You Manage Your Time?

flit - *v.* change task/job frequently and only do the job rather superficially

get rid of - *v.* remove; eliminate

hold down a job - *v.* keep your job

50 Are You a Risk Taker?

package holiday - *n.* organized holiday via an agency

resort - *n.* frequently visited tourist location

dull - *adj.* lacking in liveliness or interest

be warned - *v.* be careful

go too far - *exp.* go beyond a norm in opinion or actions

51 How Ethical Are You?

civil servant - *n.* a person working in the public administration

performance-related pay - *n.* salary in relation to how well you carry out responsibilities at work

47 Do You Have Effective Meeting Skills?

The following *scenarios* all have four possible solutions. Rank each solution in order from 1 (the best) to 4 (the least likely of success).

1. You arrive early and find the meeting room is arranged differently from what you would like. Do you?

    a) Phone the person responsible for the room and have it rearranged.
    b) Rearrange the room yourself.
    c) Wait until participants begin to arrive and ask someone to help you rearrange things.
    d) Leave the room as it is and complain later to the person responsible.

2. You expect 10 participants at a 9.00 am meeting. It is 9.05 and only eight participants are present. No one has advised you of plans to arrive late. Do you?

    a) Begin the meeting with those present.
    b) Phone the two missing people to see if they are coming.
    c) Wait another five minutes and then begin.
    d) Ask those present to vote on whether to begin now or later.

3. Some participants are not contributing to the meeting although they appear to be listening. Do you?

    a) Monitor the situation to see if it continues.
    b) Ask a non-contributing participant for an opinion or reaction.
    c) Ask the non-contributing participants why they are not involved.
    d) Do nothing – they'll speak up if they want to.

4. You get a question you can't answer. Do you?

    a) Redirect the question to the group.
    b) Ignore the question.
    c) Ask the person who asked the question why he or she asked it.
    d) Admit you don't know the answer and move on.

5. The group is getting away from the objective of the meeting. Do you?

    a) Let things continue as long as everyone seems interested.
    b) Interrupt and bring the group back to the agenda.
    c) Interrupt and vote on whether or not to continue this discussion.
    d) Take a break so participants can continue the discussion in their own time and meet again when it is over.

6. Two people, sitting together, keep *whispering* to each other. It has been going on for some time. You find it distracting. Do you?

    a) Ask them to share their discussion with the group.
    b) Ask them a content-related question to see if they have been listening.
    c) Stop talking and look at them.
    d) Ignore it and hope they finish soon.

> **SCORE**
>
> The recommended order of ranking for effective meetings is as follows:
>
> 1) a c b d
>
> 2) a c b d
>
> 3) a b c d
>
> 4) a d c b
>
> 5) b c a d
>
> 6) c b a d
>
> Clearly the more often you choose the best solution, the more effective you are in managing and taking part in meetings.

48 Are You a Good Negotiator?

1 Your child wants an increase in *pocket money* as he/she says all his/her friends get more than he/she does. Do you:

   a) refuse on principal
   b) agree but suggest that he/she does a few *household chores* in return
   c) check with other parents before you agree

2 You are in a very expensive shop and you see something you really want but you don't have enough money. Do you:

   a) stop wasting time and leave the shop
   b) ask the assistant if there's any chance of a discount
   c) go and get some more money

3 Your work colleague asks you a big favor which you *would rather* not do. Do you:

   a) refuse and explain your position
   b) agree provided they agree to do something for you later on
   c) agree but complain about it later

4 Your boss keeps giving you his/her work to do when he/she goes on holiday. Do you:

   a) ask if anyone else can do it
   b) do it happily and then ask for promotion
   c) do it because you have no choice

5 You are on your way to an important meeting but your flight has been delayed four hours. Do you:

   a) cancel your meeting and make a formal complaint to the airline
   b) ask for an upgrade to first class as compensation for the delay
   c) wait in the lounge and do some work

6 You have just been offered a *top job* but you are not happy with the salary. Do you:

   a) turn down the offer and look else where
   b) explain to your prospective employer why you are worth more
   c) accept the job and hope for a pay rise

7 You have just bought a new computer which doesn't work when you get it home. Do you:

   a) take it back and ask for a refund
   b) ask the vendor for a discount and to come and fix it at home
   c) take it back and exchange it for another one

8 You are on a business trip and the hotel room you are staying in is noisy and dirty. Do you:

   a) write a formal complaint and check out immediately
   b) complain and ask for a discount
   c) *put up with it* and then forget to make a formal complaint

9 You have a lot of building work to be done to your house but you are worried about how long it might take and how much it will cost. Do you:

   a) decide not to have the work done until you can definitely afford it
   b) make sure you get a *fixed rate deal* with the builders
   c) accept whichever builder gives the lowest *quote*

SCORE

2 points for A's, 3 for B's and 1 for C's.

21-27

You recognise the opportunity for negotiation everywhere, at home, shopping and at work! If you achieve what you attempt to, you should be a great success.

15-20

You are decisive and assertive but not a negotiator. Try to be a bit more flexible sometimes, you never know what it might lead to!

9-14

Oh dear! You need to stop letting people *trample* all over you.

49 How Well Do You Manage Your Time?

Part 1

Choose the most appropriate answer to questions 1-7.

1 Do you try to complete one job at a time, instead of *flitting* from task to task?

   a) always
   b) usually
   c) occasionally
   d) seldom

2 Do you feel there are not enough hours in a day to do what you want?

   a) very frequently
   b) generally
   c) often
   d) rarely

3 Do you review your objectives and goals with your boss?

   a) once a month
   b) quite regularly
   c) a couple of times a year
   d) never

4 When someone has done work for you incorrectly, do you correct it yourself and say nothing?

   a) as a general rule
   b) only if strictly necessary
   c) never

5 When casual visitors drop in your office, do you have difficulty *getting rid* of them?

   a) nearly always
   b) more often than not
   c) not that often
   d) extremely rarely

6 Do you take care not to over-extend your coffee and lunch breaks?

   a) whenever possible
   b) generally speaking
   c) not usually

7 Do you keep your desk clear of all papers except those you are working on?

   a) most of the time
   b) not much of the time

Part 2

Answer yes or no to the following questions.

8 Do you have a regular time each day for dealing with correspondence?
9 Do you know what you want to be doing in five years' time?
10 Do you know what time of day you work most effectively and therefore use this for working on your most difficult tasks?

SCORE

Score one point for every 'yes' to questions 1, 3, 4, 5, 6, 9, 10 and one point for every 'no' to questions 2, 7, 8.

10-8: You are very much in control of your working life - ask for an immediate rise in salary.

7-5: You need to take more care in setting your priorities, otherwise your performance is going to suffer.

4-0: You don't have a clear idea of how to organize your time - it's amazing you can *hold down* your job. Have you thought about asking for help?

50 Are You a Risk Taker?

Answer 'yes' or 'no' to the following:

1. You have never driven at more than 140 kph.
2. Your ideal job offer would be a steady, salaried position with a pension scheme.
3. You feel most comfortable when the people around you are dressed similarly.
4. You think insurance schemes are always essential.
5. You often go on *package holidays* to popular *resorts*.
6. You keep all your documents in a safe place.
7. If you won a lot of money, you would put most of it in a savings account.
8. You always check the weather forecasts.
9. You rarely do spontaneous and last minute things.
10. You would never consider working in another country.
11. You never disagree with your boss.
12. You always prepare well for meetings.
13. You would never buy shares in hi-tech companies.
14. You have more than one anti-virus program on your PC.
15. You don't give credit card details over the web.
16. You rarely try different exotic sounding foods.
17. You always make back-ups of files.
18. You hardly ever arrive at a hotel without having booked.
19. You never use the Internet at work for personal use.
20. At work you never say you've done something when in reality you haven't done it.

SCORE

MOSTLY YES'S

Your life is safe and secure but perhaps a little *dull*. Perhaps you should consider doing something a little risky as it would definitely make things a bit more interesting.

MOSTLY NO'S

You like to live an eventful and interesting life but *be warned*, one day you might just *go too far*. A few safe decisions in your life could do you some good.

YES'S AND NO'S

You are a good balance of risk taker and perfectionist. You should be successful in your life as you're both reliable and dynamic.

51 How Ethical Are You?

Choose what you think is the most appropriate answer.

1 You are a *civil servant* and arrive at your office late due to bad traffic to find several people waiting for you on routine business. One of these is a relative of yours.
   a) you deal with your relative first, even if many of the people arrived before him/her
   b) you see people in the order that they came

2 You are a manager and have some software to monitor every call that is made on your company's phones. You find yourself listening to a personal phone call.
   a) you take notes and use them for office gossip
   b) you stop listening immediately and later, if necessary, ask the person not to make personal calls again

3 You are away on business with a colleague. You see them at your host's desk reading some confidential research on some new equipment.
   a) you quickly make a photocopy
   b) you are tempted to read it but decide not to

4 You have just heard some news that annual sales figures are slightly down. This could affect your *performance-related pay*. You have to produce a report for your manager.
   a) you alter some figures so your performance looks better
   b) you present all the figures as accurately as possible

5 You are being interviewed to do some work for which you don't have much experience. You want the job very much.
   a) you invent some information about a few related jobs you've done in the past
   b) you explain how you have a lot of talents which compensate for your lack of experience

SCORE

ALL A'S:

You are an honest person and a credit both to yourself and to your company.

ONE B OR MORE

You are not a very trustworthy person.

ALL B'S

You should be in prison!

Chapter 11
Managerial Skills

In this chapter all the glossaries are listed together below.

52 Do You Have Managerial Potential?

say what's on your mind - *exp.* express what you really think about something

53 Would You Be an Ethical Leader?

sticks and stones may break my bones - *exp.* your violence could affect me physically, but nothing that you say to me will injure me

the end justifies the means - *exp.* a good outcome excuses any wrongs committed to achieve it

entrepreneur - *n.* someone who organizes a business venture and assumes the risk for it

tread on - *v.* treat badly so that you can continue on your chosen course of action

call into question - *exp.* dispute the subject matter at issue

ecological - *adj.* characterized by the interdependence of living organisms in an environment

take the initiative - *exp.* show readiness to embark on new ventures

fair - *adj.* just; acceptable

54 Would You Make a Good Manager?

praise - *v.* compliment someone who has done something of merit

work out - *v.* find, investigate

55 How Well Does Your Boss Know You?

sarcastic - *adj.* expressing ridicule

spice - *n.* something more interesting than what is currently available

bounce back - *v.* return to normality after some negative event

56 Do You Have a Manager's Approach to Work?

stick to something - *v.* continue on a course of action without being tempted to give up

awareness - *n.* inner knowledge

tackle - *v.* accept as a challenge and deal with

challenging - *adj.* requiring full use of your abilities or resources

to-do list - *n.* a list of tasks to be completed

outcome - *n.* result

pointer - *n.* indicator

take a stand against *exp.* oppose

thrive *v.* need and enjoy

praise - *n.* expression of approval and commendation

merit - *n.* admirable quality or attribute

touch - *v.* affect on an emotional or intellectual level

line of duty - *n.* acting in conformity with your responsibilities

show up for - *v.* be present at

make the grade - *exp.* be of a sufficiently high standard

52 Do You Have Managerial Potential?

Below is a list of items that discriminate between those managers who are rated as highly successful by their bosses, peers and staff, and those managers who are not viewed as particularly successful. These items were part of a large study carried out in the US by Wendy Williams and Robert Sternberg.

To see if you have managerial potential, mark the statements true (T) or false (F).

1. I think a good manager should know how to do the jobs of everyone who works for him or her.
2. I do not make decisions until I know every fact and figure.
3. When I see my boss about a problem, I describe the situation and wait for her to propose a solution.
4. I believe that some problems simply cannot be solved.
5. Instead of telling my employees all about my goals and expectations, I tell them purely what they need to know in order to do their job.
6. I act on most issues and make most decisions on my own without consulting my boss.
7. I state my opinion on issues fully and honestly – I say *what's on my mind*.
8. I make my own rules and do things my own way.
9. When dealing with people from outside the company on work issues, I am honest about my company's situation.
10. I make most decisions quickly.

SCORE

Successful managers disagreed with statements 1-5, and agreed with statements 6-10.

53 Would You Be an Ethical Leader?

Below are some commonly used proverbs and idioms in English. Decide which ones you agree with.

1. He who hesitates is lost.
2. Everyone has their price.
3. There's no pleasure without pain.
4. Money makes the world go around.
5. *The end justifies the means.*
6. Imagination is a poor substitute for experience.
7. It is better to know something about everything than everything about something.
8. Never judge someone from their clothes.
9. *Sticks and stones may break my bones but words will never hurt me.*
10. You cannot change human nature.

> SCORE
>
> If you agree with statements 1-5, you might become a very successful *entrepreneur* but you will *tread* on a lot of people on the way up, be very unscrupulous, and probably adopt environmentally unsustainable business practices.
>
> Statements 6-10 are highly subjective, but many experts would agree with statements 7 and 8, but *call into question* statements 6, 9 and 10.
>
> An ethical leader is like to have the following characteristics (these are in no particular order).
>
> Ethical leaders ...
>
> - lead by example
> - aim to produce products and services that are sustainable from an environmental and *ecological* point of view
> - are honest both with themselves and with the people they lead
> - encourage members of their team to *take the initiative* and to work together
> - have a great sense of what is *fair* and just irrespective of age, gender, ethnicity, nationality, or any other factor
> - respect others and value their contributions

54 Would You Make a Good Manager?

1 When communicating with your staff, what is most important? Being a good:

   a) listener b) speaker c) writer

2 You have just been given a new project to manage. Which is your most important role?

   a) motivating the team b) setting team objectives c) establishing rules and regulations

3 In managing relations with employees, is it better to tell them

   a) everything b) only what you think they need to know c) nothing

4 Most management decisions are based on:

   a) intuition b) hard facts c) pressure from higher levels

5 On an average day, what should a manager spend the most time doing?

   a) supporting and *praising* team members b) *working out* ways to improve efficiency c) finding errors

6 The end justifies the means:

   a) rarely b) generally c) always

7. What is the right ratio between staying at your desk and walking around the office getting feedback?

   a) 30:70 b) 60:40 c) 90:10

8 How much of being a good manager comes from qualifications and training rather than experience?

   a) 20% b) 50% c) 75%

SCORE

According to many US business gurus, the fundamental role of a manager is to be constantly in touch with his / her team and to motivate and support them. Such qualities derive from experience rather than training. So, following this approach to management, score one point for each a).

7-8: You are heading for a top managerial position.

5-6: You would make a reasonably good middle manager.

3-4: You may make project leader, but you are unlikely to get good results.

0-2: Don't choose management.

55 How Well Does Your Boss Know You?

How do you think your boss answer the following statements in relation to you? Answer 'yes' or 'no'.

1. I tend to be *envious* of the success of others.
2. I never make *sarcastic* remarks about other people.
3. I tend to leave things to the last minute.
4. I tend to find many people boring and can predict exactly what they are going to say.
5. I tend to let the escalator carry me rather than walking myself.
6. I believe that an element of risk adds *spice* to life.
7. I like to make my own decisions regardless of what other people say.
8. I find it pointless to plan things way in advance as they always tend to change.
9. I am never persuaded by illogical arguments.
10. I help others whether they help me or not.
11. I can listen to others without interrupting them.
12. I don't enjoy having to make decisions.
13. If something goes wrong for me I always *bounce back*.
14. I am concerned about what other people think about me.

SCORE

There is no score for this test.

56 Do You Have a Manager's Approach to Work?

Answer 'yes' or 'no' to the following questions.

1. Achieving my aims, however long it takes, is very important to me.
2. Acquiring knowledge for its own sake has long-term benefits.
3. After I have done something important, I still feel I could have done better.
4. Being able to develop a plan and *stick to* it is the most important part of every project.
5. Being organized is more important to me than being adaptable.
6. Generally speaking, once I've made a decision I know it's the right one.
7. I am often motivated to work by thoughts of long-term *outcomes*.
8. I enjoy working in situations involving competition with others.
9. I feel that I have an accurate *awareness* of my own abilities.
10. I like the kind of work that requires attention to detail.
11. I see a piece of work as consisting of a number of stages.
12. I tend to *tackle* a problem by separating it into its smaller component parts.
13. I tend to think about the positive rather than the negative consequences when I'm considering a course of action.
14. I usually think about a problem or piece of work for some time before actually starting in on it.
15. I would not change the way I do things just in order to please someone or win their favor.
16. I would rather do something at which I feel confident and relaxed than something which is *challenging* and difficult.
17. I'm attracted by the idea of spending a lot of time researching a project or piece of work.
18. It annoys me when other people perform better than I do.
19. It is important for me to do work as well as I can, even if it isn't popular with my co-workers.
20. It is sometimes hard for me to go on with my work if I am not encouraged.
21. Keeping my options open is more important than having *a to-do list*.
22. Logic is usually more important than following one's heart when it comes to making important decisions.
23. Part of my enjoyment in doing things is improving my past performance.
24. The most useful feedback on my work is that which gives me *pointers* for the future.
25. Work-related ideas often run through my head so that I cannot sleep.

SCORE

MAINLY YES

You fully believe in where you, your job and your company are going. You know how you to get what you want, and you prove this every day by consistently seeking to do the right thing. You like to find out what your colleagues and your bosses are thinking, the direction they are planning to go in. And if you don't agree with that direction or with a particular decision, you may occasionally *take a stand against* it. You arrive at work energetic and enthusiastic and immediately set yourself a goal for the day. You have high expectations for yourself. You *thrive* on learning new things and constantly search for greater success.

If you do not already hold a managerial position, you soon will.

A MIX OF YES AND NO

You do not yet have a clear idea of what your company culture is about: the company, its customers, its mission. As a consequence you spend some of your time simply working for yourself rather than for something greater than yourself. You react well to *praise* and recognize the *merit* in others, but it doesn't really *touch* you and you don't display any great interpersonal skills. As a result you are not particularly productive, but occasionally surprise both yourself and your company with a great idea.

You make may lower management position, but are unlikely to progress further.

MAINLY NO

You don't really feel part of your company. You hesitate to voice your opinions or feelings in either a group setting or in private. If something doesn't fall in the *line of your duty*, you tend not to do it. You are also someone who may be reluctant to follow instructions. You do not happily accept any task or project, and your goal is simply to get by rather than try to exceed expectations. Although you may derive some joy from the time you spend with your co-workers and superiors, your main motivator to work is money. The longer you work for your current company, the less likely you are to *show up for* work on time and to keep deadlines.

You have no plans to become a manager, and even if you had, you would be highly unlikely to *make the grade*.

Chapter 12
Miscellaneous

In this chapter all the glossaries are listed together below.

57 What Are Your Daily Habits?

blush - *v.* when your face turns red in embarrassment or shame

irritated - *adj.* aroused to impatience or anger

annoyed - *adj.* bothered by petty annoyances

grind your teeth - *exp.* crunch/rub together your teeth

nightmare *n.* unpleasant dream

trouble - *n.* in a bad situation that you have created yourself

mirror - *n.* polished surface that reflects your image back to you

stretched out - *adj.* with your muscles extended

folded *adj.* with your arms placed inside each other

briskly - *adv.* quickly

wash up - *v.* clean the dishes

58 How Mature Are You?

commitment *n.* something that you have agreed to do (either for yourself or others)

weigh - *v.* take into account; balance

ton of stuff - *n.* with considerable knowledge about a lot of subjects

inner journey - *n.* a journey of self exploration with the ultimate goal of knowing yourself better and thereby improving your life in general

core - *n.* the essential part

be lacking in - *v.* not having a sufficient amount of

59 Are You Caught in the Web?

addiction - *n.* an abnormally strong desire due to being dependent on something that is psychologically or physically habit-forming

quorum (plural: quorums or quora) *n.* online discussion group

trading - *n.* buying or selling securities or commodities

cyberspace - *n.* a worldwide network of computer networks

obsessed - *adj.* showing excessive or compulsive concern with something

60 Are You a Sensible Shopper?

load - *n.* a large amount of

stick to - *v.* continue as you have always done

hardwearing - *adj.* long lasting

refund - *n.* money returned to a payer

61 What Class of Airplane Passenger Are You?

There is no glossary for this test.

57 What Are Your Daily Habits?

Rate how regularly you do the following: always, usually, often, sometimes, rarely, never.

Note: There is no specific score for this test. The test is simply designed to help you learn some very every day vocabulary.

1. *Blush.*
2. Clear up and clean the house when you know guests are coming.
3. Cook meals for the others.
4. Dream that you are falling.
5. Get really *irritated* when you're working hard and concentrating on something.
6. Get so *annoyed* that you break something.
7. *Grind your teeth.*
8. Have *nightmares.*
9. Iron your clothes.
10. Keep quiet if you are in *trouble.*
11. Laugh loudly when someone says something that amuses you.
12. Leave your bed unmade.
13. Leave the lights on when you leave a room.
14. Look in the *mirror* before leaving the house.
15. Show impatience with family members who do not do things in the way you think they should be done.
16. Sit with your legs *stretched out* straight.
17. Spend a long time in the bathroom.
18. Stand with your arms *folded* when talking to people.
19. Walk briskly with long steps.
20. *Wash up.*

58 How Mature Are You?

How true are the following statements of you? a) very b) quite c) not very

1. I am fully aware of my own strengths and weaknesses.
2. I am able to keep long-term *commitments*.
3. I *weigh* the possible consequences of a future action that I might take and think about how this action might affect others.
4. I am able to see things from more than just my own point of view.
5. I am genuinely happy for the successes of others.
6. I am aware of how little I understand about certain situations.
7. I tend to save more than I spend.
8. I know when patience is called for, and I am able to apply it.
9. I try not take things too personally and to be objective.
10. Even if I don't agree with someone, I remain civil.
11. I can learn from mistakes.
12. I don't have a problem admitting that I am wrong
13. I tend not to immediately opt for easy solutions, as I prefer to look for long-term solutions.
14. I am able to respect other people, even if they offend me or I do not like them for some reason.
15. I recognize my limits.

SCORE

Becoming a mature person is, or should be, a key aspiration for everyone. Maturity is not simply acquired with age: an elderly person is not necessarily mature, and a person who knows a *ton of stuff* is not necessarily mature.

Maturity is not merely related to our experiences of life. Instead it has a relationship with our *inner journey*, with the experiences of our inner life. The more you look within yourself, the more you increases your level of maturity. Only when you have reached the very *core* of your being, will you really be mature.

Emotional intelligence and maturity, are closely linked. A mature person has better emotional skills, knows himself / herself well, and thus has the tools even to access the feelings of others by establishing empathy, i.e. the capacity to decide what to do and what not to do, taking into account not only your own instincts, but also of people and situations that you have around you.

MOSTLY A'S

You have already reached a very high level of maturity and are likely to command the respect, love and admiration of those around you.

MOSTLY B'S

You are still on your journey to maturity, with time and experience helping you on your way.

MOSTLY C'S

You are clearly *lacking* in confidence and really need to understand yourself better.

59 Are You Caught in the Web?

Test your level of *addiction* to the Internet.

Rate yourself using this scale

0 = not true at all   1 = quite true   2 = very true

1. You are constantly shopping online.
2. You always book your plane tickets over the web.
3. You often stay on the web longer than you had intended.
4. You always check your social media notifications first thing in the morning.
5. Your work suffers because of the amount of time you spend navigating.
6. You have more 'virtual' friends than you have 'real' friends.
7. You spend many evenings a week taking part in chat rooms or answering questions in *quorums*.
8. You pass a lot of time at auctions or *trading* online.
9. Your family complain about how much time you spend in front of the screen.
10. If you are honest with yourself, you prefer *cyberspace* to the real world.

SCORE

15-20

You live very much a virtual life. Think of the possible psychological damage that this may be causing you.

10-14

You are two steps from becoming *obsessed* with the cyber world - get a life!

6-10

You have a practical sense of what the web has to offer.

0-5

You live very much in the real world and have decided to reject much of what the web has to offer.

60 Are You a Sensible Shopper?

1. You go into a clothing store. Do you?

   a. Buy exactly what it was you were looking for and no more.
   b. Come out with far more than you had planned to buy.

2. You are looking for something on Amazon. Do you?

   a. Click away and not worry too much about the cost of your trolley.
   b. Keep a careful note of what you put in your trolley.

3. You are in a supermarket. Do you?

   a. Buy a whole *load* of items just because they are on special offer.
   b. *Stick* to what you really need.

4. When buying something at the supermarket. Do you?

   a. Always check the price of similar products before making a decision.
   b. Never even look at the price tag.

5. When purchasing a new pair of shoes, what are your main criteria? The shoes should be:

   a. Fashionable.
   b. The right size and *hardwearing*.

6. When buying food, do you always look at the sell-buy date?

   a. Yes.
   b. No.

7. When you have bought an electrical item do you always keep the guarantee and archive it?

   a. Yes.
   b. No.

8. Do you tend to buy items at stores where they offer to *refund* you if you are not satisfied with your purchase?

   a. Yes.
   b. No.

SCORE

Sensible: 1 a, 2 b, 3 b, 4 a, 5 b, 6 a, 7 a, 8 a

Rather irresponsible: 1 b, 2 a, 3 a, 4 b, 5 a, 6 b, 7 b, 8 b

61 What Class of Airplane Passenger Are You?

1 Do you talk to the person sitting next to you?

   a Always. I like to spend the whole journey chatting.
   b Only if he/she wants to chat.
   c I prefer not to.

2 What is your opening sentence likely to be?

   a Are you travelling on business?
   b Do you mind if I look at your newspaper?
   c Do you speak English?

3 How much noise do you make during the flight?

   a A lot especially when I turn the pages of my newspaper.
   b I'm as quiet as a mouse.
   c It depends on what music and movies I have on my phone.

4 How much do you eat and drink during your flight?

   a As much as possible.
   b Very little as I hate disturbing other people when I go to the toilet.
   c It depends on the quality.

5 How nervous are you during takeoff and landing?

   a Very, I need a lot of reassurance from the cabin crew.
   b Generally I don't notice either.
   c It depends on how old the plane looks.

6 What items are you likely to carry with you?

   a Tablet, magazines, newspapers.
   b Just an umbrella if I'm going to the UK.
   c A face mask and ear plugs.

7 How well do you sleep on planes?

   a Sometimes I sleep but I also snore.
   b Very well thank you.
   c It depends on the person sitting next to me.

SCORE

PREDOMINANTLY A'S

You are a nightmare to sit next to on a plane. You make too much noise, talk too much, and may also be quite nervous.

PREDOMINANTLY B'S

You are the ideal person to sit next to on a plane. You don't want to disturb anyone - neither the person next to you or the other passengers.

PREDOMINANTLY C'S

You are a good person to sit next to. You keep yourself to yourself when necessary, but are also happy to have a conversation where appropriate.

Appendix 1

Alphabetical Glossary of the Whole Book

Below is a glossary in alphabetical order of all the words and expressions that are highlighted in italics in Chapters 1-12. This glossary is then followed in Appendix 2 by vocabulary tests grouped by the grammatical part of speech (noun, verb, adjective).

accomplish	*v.* gain with effort
addiction	*n.* an abnormally strong desire due to being dependent on something that is psychologically or physically habit-forming
addictive	*adj.* making you unable to stop (typically of a bad habit)
adverse	*adj.* contrary to your interests
advice	*n.* a proposal for an appropriate course of action
aid	*v.* help
Airbnb	*n.* online marketplace and homestay network enabling people to list or rent short-term accommodation in residential properties
alienate	*v.* arouse indifference or hostility in where there had formerly been harmony, understanding, affection, or friendliness
allure	*v.* entice or attract through personal charm
anecdote	*n.* short account of an incident
annoyed	*adj.* bothered by petty annoyances
anxiety	*n.* unpleasant emotion that is experienced in anticipation of some (usually ill-defined) misfortune
application	*n.* request for employment or admission to a school/college
argument	*n.* heated discussion (i.e. where there is strong disagreement)
ask someone out	*v.* find out whether someone is interested in having a relationship by asking them if they would like to go out for a drink, go to the cinema with you etc.
assignment	*n.* exercise, task, essay
autonomy	*n.* independence

aware	*adj.* having or showing knowledge or understanding; conscious; attentive to
awareness	*n.* inner knowledge
back of your mind (be at the)	*exp.* a feeling or thought that is constantly with you
bargain	*n.* an advantageous purchase
bark	*v.* the loud noise made by a dog
be better off	*exp.* be in a better position/situation
be dealt a bad hand	*exp.* be given a series of negative factors to deal with
be lacking in	*v.* not having a sufficient amount of
be supposed to	*v.* be (mistakenly) believed; commonly put forth or accepted as true on inconclusive grounds
be warned	*v.* be careful
bear a grudge	*exp.* maintain resentment or anger against someone for a past offense
bedraggled	*adj.* in a very bad condition
beggar	*n.* a poor person who lives by asking people in the street for money or food
beneath	*adv.* under
billboard	*n.* advertising space found alongside roads
bitter	*adj.* marked by strong resentment or cynicism
blame	*v.* attribute the responsibility to someone for something that has gone wrong
blast	*v.* play music at a very high volume
bloated	*adj.* with a very full stomach
blush	*v.* when your face turns red in embarrassment or shame
bonds, stocks, shares	*n.* forms of financial investment
border	*n.* boundary between two nations
bounce back	*v.* return to normality after some negative event
boundary	*n.* a limit past which people should not cross
brass band	*n.* orchestra that plays brass instruments (i.e. wind instruments that consist of a brass tube)
breathless	*adj.* able to breathe only with difficulty
bright side of life (look on the)	*exp.* always see the positive aspects of a situation
briskly	*adv.* quickly
broadcaster	*noun* someone who transmits a program or some information on radio or television
bulldozing	*adj.* aggressive
bullfight	*n.* spectacle where a matador baits and (usually) kills a bull in an arena before many spectators
bullying	*n.* act of intimidating a weaker person to make them do something
burden	*n.* load, weight
burp	*v.* expel wind noisily from the stomach through the mouth
bury	*v.* place a dead person in a grave
butcher	*n.* a person who slaughters meat for market; someone who sells meat from a shop
buzzing	*adj.* noisy like the sound of a bee

call into question	*exp.* dispute the subject matter at issue
captivated	*adj.* filled with wonder and delight
cardigan	*n.* knitted jacket that is fastened up the front with buttons or a zipper
casino	*n.* place for gambling and entertainment
cast one's vote	*v.* officially express your preference for a particular candidate or option
challenging	*adj.* requiring full use of your abilities or resources
charades	*n.* game in which participants act out a phrase for others to guess
charity	*n.* an institution set up to provide help to the needy; a foundation created to promote the public good
charity flag day	*n.* an activity to raise money for an institution set up to provide help to the needy
cheap and cheerful	*exp.* despite not being expensive, an object or place that is sufficiently pleasant
check up on	*v.* investigate, verify
cheer up	*v.* become more content after being sad
cheer yourself up	*v.* make yourself feel happier after a negative event
cheery	*adj.* bright and pleasant; promoting a feeling of cheer
chess	*n.* an ancient board game for two players who move their 16 pieces according to specific rules
chuckle	*v.* laugh quietly or with restraint
civil servant	*n.* a person working in the public administration
civil service	*n.* public administration, government work
clapping	*n.* a demonstration of approval by repeatedly putting your hands together to make a noise
come out on top	*v.* get very good results, better than others
comfort zone	*n.* a situation where you feel safe and at ease
comfortable	*adj.* free from stress, accepting
commission	*n.* fee for services rendered based on a percentage of an amount received or collected or agreed to be paid (as distinguished from a salary)
commitment	*n.* something that you have agreed to do (either for yourself or others)
company profile	*n.* sketch/analysis representing the extent to which a company exhibits various characteristics
compatible	*adj.* able to exist and perform in harmonious or agreeable combination
conscious reasoning	*n.* thinking that is coherent and logical
consistency	*n.* always following the same logic and behavior
continental breakfast	*n.* in British English used to specify a (simple) breakfast that is typical of Europe as opposed to the characteristic 'full English breakfast'
continuum	*n.* succession in which no one part is distinct or distinguishable from another
convenient	*adj.* suitable
cope	*v.* come to terms or deal successfully with
core	*n.* the essential part; heart
count	*v.* rely on
create a fuss	*v.* create a state of agitation or an angry disturbance
critical thinking	*n.* the process of using your mind to consider something carefully
crop up	*v.* take place, occur, happen

croupier	*n.* someone who collects and pays bets at a gaming table
crowdfunding	*n.* practice of funding a project or venture by raising monetary contributions from a large number of people
curse word	*n.* offensive word used to express anger or annoyance
cut corners	*exp.* not complete tasks as they should be, not act in a proper way
cut off	*v.* . end
cyberspace	*n.* a worldwide network of computer networks
dare	*n.* a challenge to do something dangerous
day dream	*n.* thoughts about things you'd like to do, or places where you'd like to be, or people you'd like to be with
decline	*v.* refuse politely
decorating	*n.* painting and furnishing your house/flat/room
defy	*v.* go against
deja vu	*n.* a feeling of having been somewhere or done something before
deluded	*adj.* believing that you have a particular quality when in fact you probably don't
demure	*adj.* affectedly modest or shy especially in a playful or provocative way
deny	*v.* declare untrue
destroy	*v.* damage irreparably
dexterity	*n.* very good at using one's hands
digestible	*adj.* capable of being understood
discredited	*adj.* no longer accepted; brought into disrepute
discreet	*adj.* unobtrusive
disposition	*n.* your usual mood
diurnal	*adj.* occurring every day
do your bit	*exp.* make your contribution
domestic chores	*n.* cleaning and tidying activities around the house
drama	*n.* a highly (and probably unnecessarily) emotional episode
drawer	*n.* a box-like container in a piece of furniture
dreadful	*adj.* exceptionally bad or displeasing
dull	*adj.* lacking in liveliness or interest
ear plugs	*n.* device to put in your ears to stop external sound from penetrating your ears
early bird	*n.* someone who gets up very early in the morning
ecological	*adj.* characterized by the interdependence of living organisms in an environment
edge	*n.* limit
elderly	*adj.* advanced in years
energize	*v.* inject with energy
energy draining	*adj.* lowering your levels of energy
enhance	*v.* increase; make better or more attractive
enlisted soldier	*n.* man or woman who serves in an army
enrolled	*adj.* registered
entail	*v.* involve
entrepreneur	*n.* someone who organizes a business venture and assumes the risk for it
equate	*v.* be equivalent, similar, equal, or analogous to something else
exotic	*adj.* characteristic of another (apparently more exciting) place or part of the world

Appendix 1

extra-terrestrial	*n.* a creature from another planet
face up to	*exp.* address a problem and try to deal with it
failure	*n.* the opposite of success
fair	*adj.* just; acceptable
fair amount	*exp.* adequate; considerable quantity
fairly	*adv.* to a moderately sufficient extent or degree
fairy godmother	*n.* someone imaginary who helps you when you are in a difficult situation
fancy dress party	*n.* party where people wear costumes
figment of the imagination	*n.* a contrived or fantastic idea
fill someone with delight	*exp.* provide a feeling of extreme pleasure or satisfaction
fire practice	*n.* the act of simulating and preparing for a possible fire
firefighter	*n.* a member of a fire department who tries to extinguish fires
fixed rate deal	*n.* amount of a charge or payment that is established at the beginning of a job to be done and which binds the party providing the service
flag someone down	*v.* stand at a roadside attempting to stop a passing car in order to be helped
flights (of stairs)	*n.* section of a staircase between one floor and another
flit	*v.* change task/job frequently and only do the job rather superficially
flu	*n.* common and contagious viral disease (short form of 'influenza')
flustered	*adj.* thrown into a state of agitated confusion
folded	*adj.* with your arms placed inside each other
fool yourself	*v.* give yourself the wrong impression
foul	*adj.* unpleasant
fraud	*n.* deliberate dishonest behavior intended to gain an advantage
fret	*v.* worry
fruit machine	*n.* mechanical device for gambling, typically found in bars, cinemas
fulfilled	*adj.* satisfied
fun fair	*n.* amusement park
gamble	*v.* play games for money; take a risk in the hope of a favorable outcome
gambling	*n.* the act of playing for stakes (money) in the hope of winning
gentle	*adj.* having or showing a kindly or tender nature
get away with	*v.* manage to do something without any of the foreseen negative consequences
get by	*v.* manage, succeed
get on well with	*v.* have a good relationship with
get rid of	*v.* remove; eliminate
get someone down	*v.* disappoint, make sad/depressed
ghost	*n.* supernatural appearance of a dead person
gift	*n.* a present
give credit when credit is due	*exp.* recognize an achievement when it deserves praise
glide	*v.* move smoothly and effortlessly
go blind	*v.* enter a situation with your eyes closed, i.e. without really thinking about what you are doing
go into the red	*exp.* go under the permitted amount on your bank account

go too far	*exp.* go beyond a norm in opinion or actions
gossip	*n.* light informal (but potentially malicious) conversation for social occasions
gossip	*v.* speak about others behind their back and reveal secrets or intimacies
grind your teeth	*exp.* crunch/rub together your teeth
guilty	*adj.* feeling responsible for something that you have done (or not done)
gut reaction	*n.* immediate reaction not based on reasoning
haggle	*v.* negotiate over a price, terms of an agreement
hang on to	*v.* keep
hard wired	*adj.* genetically determined
hardwearing	*adj.* long lasting
harmless	*adj.* unlikely to harm or disturb anyone
harness	*v.* control; keep in check
haunted	*adj.* apparently inhabited by a ghost
hazard	*n.* potential danger
hell	*n.* a cause of difficulty and suffering
hence	*adv.* as a result
hideous	*adj.* extremely ugly
hiking	*n.* a long walk for exercise or pleasure
hitch	*v.* travel by getting a free ride from someone
hold down a job	*v.* keep your job
horn	*n.* a noise made by the driver of an automobile to give warning
household chores	*n.* cleaning and tidying activities around the house
human resources manager	*n.* someone in charge of a group of team of people that recruits, interviews, and trains employees as well as dealing with their individual issues
humility	*n.* the opposite of arrogance
hurl abuse	*v.* utter a rude expression intended to offend
hurry (be in a)	*v.* have a very limited amount of time
idealistic	*adj.* believing in some (possibly unattainable) morals, values and principles
impeded	*adj.* made difficult or slow
impromptu	*adj.* with little or no preparation
in a rush	*exp.* needing to do something quickly, under pressure to do something
ineffectual	*adj.* lacking in power or forcefulness
inner journey	*n.* a journey of self exploration with the ultimate goal of knowing yourself better and thereby improving your life in general
inner self	*n.* your personal, internal identity
intriguing	*adj.* capable of arousing interest or curiosity
introspective	*adj.* given to examining your sensory and perceptual experiences
intuition	*n.* instinctive knowing without the use of rational processes
intuitive	*adj.* obtained through intuition rather than from reasoning or observation
irritated	*adj.* aroused to impatience or anger
jack of all trades	*n.* someone who can conduct any kind of (manual) job
jangle	*v.* shake a metallic container (in this case a money collection tin) in order to attract attention
juicy	*adj.* suggestive of sexual impropriety
jump to conclusions	*exp.* decide something very quickly without reasoning about it

Appendix 1

just for the hell of it	*exp.* just for fun
keep something back	*v.* refrain from mentioning
keep your cool	*exp.* maintain your calm in a difficult situation
kidding (to be)	*v.* . joke
lack	*v.* be without
lend a sympathetic ear	*exp.* listen to someone with understanding and compassion
let yourself go	*v.* allow yourself to lose your inhibitions
lie	*v.* not tell the untruth
life and soul	*n.* the center of attention/energy at a social event
lifespan	*n.* the period between birth and death
line of duty	*n.* acting in conformity with your responsibilities
load	*n.* a large amount of
lobster	*n.* a large marine crustacean which is a culinary delicacy
long for	*v.* desire strongly or persistently
lounge	*n.* a sitting room in a house
lovely	*adj.* beautiful, very nice
loyal	*adj.* showing constant support for a person
lumberjack	*n.* a person who cuts down trees
make the grade	*exp.* be of a sufficiently high standard
matched (to be)	*v.* be suited
medium-rare	*adj.* cooked so that quite a bit of blood is left
mellow	*adj.* relaxed, easygoing, genial
merit	*n.* admirable quality or attribute
midwife	*n.* a woman skilled in aiding the delivery of babies
mind	*v.* be concerned and bothered with or about something or somebody
mirror	*n.* polished surface that reflects your image back to you
miserable	*adj.* very unhappy
mistake someone for someone else	*exp.* think that someone is another person
moaner	*n.* a person given to excessive complaints and crying
moronic	*adj.* ridiculous
murder	*n.* premeditated killing of a human being by another human being
navy blue	*adj.* color typical used on military ships or naval uniforms
night owl	*n.* a person who likes to be active late at night
night shift	*n.* working period that takes place at night typically in manual jobs but also in hospitals
nightmare	*n.* bad/unpleasant dream
non-verbal cues	*n.* indicators of what someone is feeling revealed through their body language rather than what they are saying
obey	*v.* do what someone tells you to do
obnoxious	*adj.* causing disapproval or protest
obsessed	*adj.* showing excessive or compulsive concern with something
oil rig	*n.* a structure with equipment for drilling an oil well; an oil platform
on the fly	*exp.* while already in progress, spontaneously
on the spur of the moment	*exp.*- spontaneously
once in a blue moon	*exp.* extremely rarely

open-minded	*adj.* ready to entertain new ideas
out-of-body experience	*n.* apparently supernatural state where you feel that you have left your body
outcome	*n.* result
outgoing	*adj.* extrovert, at ease in talking to others
outgoings	*n.* the opposite of income, i.e. money you spend on bills, household items etc.
overcharged (to be)	*v.* . to pay more than was due or expected
overly	*adv.* to an excessive degree
overqualified	*adj.* with more than a sufficient number of qualifications and thus probably unsuitable/unsuited to a particular job
overtime	*n.* work done in addition to regular working hours
package holiday	*n.* organized holiday via an agency
panic	*n.* overcome by a sudden fear
parcel	*n.* a package that has been wrapped
pastel	*adj.* delicate and pale in color
peak	*v.* to reach the highest point; attain maximum intensity
pensioner	*n.* someone who is no longer in employment and who receives money (a pension) from the state
perceived	*adj.* detected by instinct or inference
perfectionism	*n.* a disposition to feel that anything less than perfect is unacceptable
performance-related pay	*n.* salary in relation to how well you carry out responsibilities at work
pet	*n.* domestic animal (cat, dog, rabbit) typically treated like a member of the family
play	*n.* a theatrical performance
play sick	*exp.* pretend to be ill in order not to have to do something that you don't want to do
plumber	*n.* person who installs and repairs pipes and fixtures and appliances
pocket money	*n.* spending money given to a child
pointer	*n.* indicator
pointless	*adj.* serving no useful purpose
pollution	*n.* contamination with harmful substances as a consequence of human activities
pot of gold	*n.* a container full of cold that in folklore is reputedly found at the end of a rainbow
pour your heart out	*exp.* tell someone your deepest feelings in a prolonged spurt
practice what you preach	*exp.* act in accordance with how you say that you should act
praise	*n.* expression of approval and commendation
praise	*v.* compliment someone who has done something of merit
prank	*n.* joke
prescription	*n.* written instructions from a physician or dentist to a pharmacist concerning the form and dosage of a drug
prestige	*n.* a high standing achieved through success
presume	*v.* accept without verification or proof
primrose	*n.* a yellow flower
procrastinate	*v.* postpone doing what you should be doing

Appendix 1

proffer	*v.* present for acceptance or rejection
proud	*adj.* feeling good about someone close (partner, member of family, colleague) due to their very good performance
prudence	*n.* discretion in practical affairs; knowing how to avoid embarrassment or distress
prying	*adj.* too curious or inquisitive
pushy	*adj.* rather aggressive ambition
put up with something	*v.* cope with or manage some kind of adverse situation without actually trying to change it
put yourself in someone else's shoes	*exp.* project yourself into someone else's predicament and understand how they feel
quorum	(plural quorums or quora) *n.* online discussion group
quote	*n.* estimate of cost
rainbow	*n.* an arc of colored light in the sky caused by refraction of the sun's rays by rain
recipe	*n.* directions for making something in the kitchen
reckless	*adj.* marked by defiant disregard for danger or consequences
refund	*n.* money returned to a payer
reimburse	*v.* pay back for some expense incurred
reincarnation	*n.* doctrine/belief that person may be reborn
rely	*v.* have confidence or faith in
rely on	*v.* count on, exploit
resentful	*adj.* full of resentment and ill will
resign yourself	*v.* accept as inevitable
resigned	*adj.* having come to accept
resolution	*n.* plan to take a particular course of action
resort	*n.* frequently visited tourist location
retire	*v.* stop working because you have reached a certain age
riddle	*n.* a question or statement intentionally phrased so as to require ingenuity in ascertaining its answer or meaning
risk your shirt	*v.* undertake a venture without regard to possible loss or injury
root of all evil	*exp.* the prime cause of everything that is bad
roundabouts, carousels	*n.* rides typically chosen by young children when at a fun fair
ruin	*n.* an irrecoverable state of destruction
run	*v.* manage
sainthood	*n.* the status of a saint, i.e. a person acknowledged as holy or virtuous in the Christian faith
sarcastic	*adj.* expressing ridicule
say what's on your mind	*exp.* express what you really think about something
scenario	*n.* situation.
séance	*n.* a meeting at which people attempt to make contact with the dead,
self esteem	*n.* an attitude of admiration, approval and liking of and for oneself
selfish	*adj.* concerned only with yourself to the exclusion of others
selfless	*adj.* concerned for the welfare of others rather than your own needs
sensible	*adj.* showing reason or sound judgment
sensitive	*adj.* being susceptible to attitudes, feelings, or circumstances

set something aside	*v.* put to one side; out of the way (especially away from one's thoughts)
set yourself up	*v.* allow yourself to be in a weak position so that someone else can potentially do something negative to you
sewer	*n.* a waste pipe that carries away sewage or surface water
shaking	*v.* when your body moves involuntarily when something negative has happened to you or is about to happen
shame	*n.* a painful emotion resulting from an awareness of inadequacy
sheer	*adj.* complete and without restriction
short notice	*n.* without advance notification
short of (to be)	*exp.* to have an insufficient amount of something
show up for	*v.* be present at
shun	*v.* deliberately avoid
shyness	*n.* a feeling of fear of embarrassment
sit out	*v.* remain for the whole duration
skydiving	*n.* performing acrobatics in free fall
slot machine	*n.* a machine for gambling typical found in bars, cinemas etc.
spice	*n.* something more interesting than what is currently available
spike	*n.* sudden peak (typically found in graphs, but in this specific case used in a metaphorical sense)
spot	*v.* notice, identify
stall-holder	*n.* someone with a vending point at a market
stand	*v.* how you feel about, what your position is in relation to something
stare	*v.* . watch/observe in a fixed manner
starring (to be)	*v.* to be the most important performer or have the most important role
start up	*n.* very new enterprise/company
starter	*n.* food or drink to stimulate the appetite usually served before a meal or as the first course
stick to	*v.* continue as you have always done
stick to details	*v.* never deviate from the details
stick to something	*v.* continue on a course of action without being tempted to give up
sticks and stones may break my bones	*exp.* your violence might affect me physically, but nothing that you say to me will injure me
straightforward	*adj.* direct, free from ambiguity
stretched out	*adj.* with your muscles extended
struggle	*v.* have great difficulty
stuck	*adj.* caught; fixed
stuff	*n.* unspecified belongings
submissive	*adj.* willing to submit to orders or wishes of others
succumb	*v.* consent reluctantly
sun-drenched	*adj.* covered with sunlight
supposed to be	*v.* . to be expected to
surgeon	*n.* a physician who specializes in surgery, i.e. cutting open the human body to perform a medical intervention
survivor	*n.* someone who does not die in an accident
sympathy	*n.* sharing and understanding the negative feelings or situation of others
tackle	*v.* accept as a challenge and deal with
tactfully	*adv.* showing diplomacy
take a stand against	*exp.* oppose

Appendix 1

take something to heart	*exp.* take criticism seriously and be affected or upset by it
take something to the next level	*exp.* progress to a higher and better point/stage
take the initiative	*exp.* show readiness to embark on new ventures
take time off	*exp.* stop going to work for a limited period
taunting	*v.* abuse vocally by deriding, mocking or criticizing
tease	*v.* ridicule, harass, provoke
teasing	*n.* playful provocation
tell someone off	*v.* reprimand
teller	*n.* an employee of a bank who receives and pays out money
the end justifies the means	*exp.* a good outcome excuses any wrongs committed to achieve it
therefore	*adv.* as a consequence
think outside the box	*exp.* not to think in the usual standard way, but instead think laterally in order generate unusual approaches or solutions
thoroughly	*adv.* completely
threat	*n.* a warning that something unpleasant is imminent
threaten	*v.* express an intention that is likely to go against the wishes of the person receiving the threat
threshold	*n.* the starting point for a new state or experience (in this specific case, level of tolerance)
thrill rides at a fun fair	*n.* activities causing high levels of sensation at an amusement park
thrive	*v.* need and enjoy
ticklish spot	*n.* location on your body that is susceptible to being tickled (i.e. light touching by another person of one of the parts of your body in a way that is slightly irritating but always makes you want to laugh)
tidy	*adj.* marked by good order and cleanliness in appearance or habits
tip	*n.* money given for services rendered (e.g. in a restaurant or bar)
to-do list	*n.* a list of tasks to be completed
ton of stuff	*n.* with considerable knowledge about a lot of subjects
top job	*n.* very good job in high position
top of the range	*exp.* the best in its category
topless beach	*noun.* a sandy area near the sea where relax without a bra/the top half of a bikini
touch	*v.* affect on an emotional or intellectual level
tradesman	*n.* a merchant who owns or manages a shop
trading	*n.* buying or selling securities or commodities
trait	*n.* a distinguishing feature of your personal nature
trample over someone	*v.* let another person do whatever he/she wants even though this goes totally against your own best interests
trance	*n.* a psychological state as if induced by a magical incantation; *v.* attract; cause to be enamored
tread	*v.* crush; treat badly so that you can continue on your chosen course of action
trembling	*v.* . slight shaking
trendy	*adj.* in accord with the latest fashion
trouble	*n.* in a bad situation that you have created yourself

turn off	*n.* something unattractive
turn on	*n.* something attractive
turn out	*v.* reveal itself to be
turn out right	*exp.* have a final positive result
turn your hand at something	*exp.* be able to conduct a manual task or a job
underlying	*adj.* being or involving basic facts or principles
unscathed	*adj.* completely unharmed
up to scratch	*adj.* of expected quality
upbringing	*n.* experience acquired during a person's formative years
upset	*adj.* mildly distressed
upset	*v.* cause an emotional disturbance
vegan	*n.* someone who eats no animal or dairy products at all
wardrobe	*n.* piece of furniture that provides storage space for clothes
wash up	*v.* clean the dishes
water	*v.* salivate
weigh	*v.* take into account; balance
well done	*adj.* cooked for a sufficient to remove the redness (blood) of the meat
well-rehearsed	*adj.* practiced many times in order to be ready for something
wellbeing	*n.* a contented state of being happy, healthy and prosperous
whisper	*v.* speak softly without vibration of the vocal cords
white lie	*n.* a statement (considered of no great importance) that deviates from the truth
wise	*adj.* having good judgment or common sense in practical matters often (but not necessarily) acquired in later life
wonder	*n.* the positive feeling aroused by something strange, surprising or wonderful
work out	*v.* find
work out right	*exp.* have a final positive result
workaholic	*n.* person with a compulsive need to work
would rather	*v.* would prefer
yearn	*v.* desire, want badly
yuk	*n.* a sound/exclamation made to express disgust
yummy	*adj.* extremely pleasing to the sense of taste

Appendix 2

Vocabulary Tests

The exercises on the following pages should ideally be done when you have read the entire book and have thus learned (or at least read) the words and expressions that appear in the glossaries.

They are all matching exercises. You simply have to match the word/expression with its definition.

The tests are grouped by grammatical part of speech.

1-7 Adjectives

1

deluded	affectedly modest or shy especially in a playful or provocative way
demure	being susceptible to attitudes, feelings, or circumstances
idealistic	believing in some (possibly unattainable) morals, values and principles
obnoxious	believing that you have a particular quality when in fact you probably don't
proud	causing disapproval or protest
selfish	concerned for the welfare of others rather than your own needs
selfless	concerned only with yourself to the exclusion of others
sensitive	feeling good about yourself or someone close (partner, member of family, colleague) due to your/their very good performance

2

dull	feeling responsible for something that you have done (or not done)
gentle	full of resentment and ill will
guilty	given to examining your sensory and perceptual experiences
ineffectual	having come to accept

introspective	having good judgment or common sense in practical matters often (but not necessarily) acquired in later life
resentful	having or showing a kindly or tender nature
resigned	lacking in power or forcefulness
wise	lacking in liveliness or interest

3

fulfilled	marked by defiant disregard for danger or consequences
intuitive	obtained through intuition rather than from reasoning or observation
loyal	rather aggressive ambition
moronic	ready to entertain new ideas
open-minded	ridiculous
pushy	satisfied
reckless	showing constant support for a person

4

bulldozing	showing excessive or compulsive concern with something
discreet	showing reason or sound judgment
miserable	too curious or inquisitive
obsessed	unobtrusive
prying	very unhappy
sensible	willing to submit to orders or wishes of others
submissive	aggressive

5

annoyed	aroused to impatience or anger
bedraggled	bothered by petty annoyances
bloated	completely unharmed
captivated	filled with wonder and delight
discredited	genetically determined
flustered	in a very bad condition
folded	made difficult or slow
hard wired	no longer accepted; brought into disrepute
impeded	thrown into a state of agitated confusion
irritated	with a very full stomach
overqualified	with more than a sufficient number of qualifications and thus probably unsuitable/unsuited to a particular job
unscathed	with your arms placed inside each other

6

addictive	able to exist and perform in harmonious or agreeable combination
bitter	bright and pleasant; promoting a feeling of cheer
buzzing	characteristic of another (apparently more exciting) place or part of the world
challenging	exceptionally bad or displeasing
cheery	making you unable to stop (typically of a bad habit)
compatible	marked by strong resentment or cynicism
dreadful	noisy like the sound of a bee

Appendix 2

exotic	requiring full use of your abilities or resources
resourceful	strikingly strange or unusual; characteristic of another place or part of the world

7

foul	beautiful, very nice
hideous	capable of arousing interest or curiosity
intriguing	direct, free from ambiguity
lovely	extremely pleasing to the sense of taste
pointless	extremely ugly
straightforward	in accord with the latest fashion
tidy	marked by good order and cleanliness in appearance or habits
trendy	serving no useful purpose
yummy	unpleasant

8-11 Expressions Containing Verbs

8

back of your mind (be at the)	a feeling or thought that is constantly with you
be better off	address a problem and try to deal with it
be dealt a bad hand	adequate; considerable quantity
bear a grudge	always see the positive aspects of a situation
bright side of life (look on the)	be given a series of negative factors to deal with
call into question	be in a better position/situation
cut corners	dispute the subject matter at issue
do your bit	maintain resentment or anger against someone for a past offense
face up to	make your contribution
fair amount	not complete tasks as they should be, not act in a proper way

9

fill someone with delight	be of a sufficiently high standard
give credit when credit is due	decide something very quickly without reasoning about it
go into the red	go beyond a norm in opinion or actions
go too far	go under the permitted amount on your bank account
jump to conclusions	just for fun
just for the hell of it	listen to someone with understanding and compassion
keep your cool	maintain your calm in a difficult situation
lend a sympathetic ear	pretend to be ill in order not to have to do something that you don't want to do
make the grade	provide a feeling of extreme pleasure or satisfaction
play sick	recognize an achievement when it deserves praise
pour your heart out	tell someone your deepest feelings in a prolonged spurt

10

practice what you preach	a good outcome excuses any wrongs committed to achieve it
put yourself in someone else's shoes	act in accordance with how you say that you should act
say what's on your mind	be able to conduct a manual task or a job
the end justifies the means	express what you really think about something
think outside the box	have a final positive result
top of the range	have a final positive result
turn out right	not to think in the usual standard way, but instead think laterally in order generate unusual approaches or solutions
turn your hand at something	project yourself into someone else's predicament and understand how they feel
work out right	the best in its category

11

take a stand against	take criticism seriously and be affected or upset by it
take something to heart	progress to a higher and better point/stage
take something to the next level	show readiness to embark on new ventures
take the initiative	stop going to work for a limited period
take time off	oppose

12-15 Abstract Nouns

12

addiction	a challenge to do something dangerous
advice	a highly (and probably unnecessarily) emotional episode
argument	a proposal for an appropriate course of action
autonomy	a situation where you feel safe and at ease
awareness	an abnormally strong desire due to being dependent on something that is psychologically or physically habit-forming
comfort zone	heated discussion (i.e. where there is strong disagreement)
critical thinking	independence
dare	inner knowledge
drama	the process of using your mind to consider something carefully

13

gossip	a disposition to feel that anything less than perfect is unacceptable
humility	a high standing achieved through success
intuition	admirable quality or attribute
merit	an irrecoverable state of destruction
panic	expression of approval and commendation

Appendix 2

perfectionism	instinctive knowing without the use of rational processes
praise	light informal (but potentially malicious) conversation for social occasions
prestige	overcome by a sudden fear
ruin	the opposite of arrogance

14

self esteem	a contented state of being happy, healthy and prosperous
shame	a distinguishing feature of your personal nature
shyness	a feeling of fear of embarrassment
spice	a painful emotion resulting from an awareness of inadequacy
sympathy	a statement (considered of no great importance) that deviates from the truth
trait	an attitude of admiration, approval and liking of and for oneself
trouble	in a bad situation that you have created yourself
wellbeing	sharing and understanding the negative feelings or situation of others
white lie	something more interesting than what is currently available

15-16 People and Jobs

15

beggar	a member of a fire department who tries to extinguish fires
broadcaster	a person who slaughters meat for market; someone who sells meat from a shop
butcher	a person working in the public administration
civil servant	a poor person who lives by asking people in the street for money or food
croupier	a woman skilled in aiding the delivery of babies
entrepreneur	someone in charge of a group of team of people that recruits, interviews, and trains employees as well as dealing with their individual issues
firefighter	someone who collects and pays bets at a gaming table
human resources manager	someone who organizes a business venture and assumes the risk for it
midwife	someone who transmits a program or some information on the radio or television

16

pensioner	a merchant who owns or manages a shop
plumber	a physician who specializes in surgery, i.e. cutting open the human body to perform a medical intervention
stall-holder	an employee of a bank who receives and pays out money
surgeon	person who installs and repairs pipes and fixtures and appliances
teller	person with a compulsive need to work
tradesman	someone who eats no animal or dairy products at all
vegan	someone who is no longer in employment and who receives money (a pension) from the state
workaholic	someone with a vending point at a market

17-18 Word-Related Nouns

17

bargain	a machine for gambling typical found in bars, cinemas etc.
bonds, stocks, shares	amount of a charge or payment that is established at the beginning of a job to be done and which binds the party providing the service
charity	an advantageous purchase
commission	an institution set up to provide help to the needy; a foundation created to promote the public good
crowdfunding	deliberate dishonest behavior intended to gain an advantage
fixed rate deal	fee for services rendered based on a percentage of an amount received or collected or agreed to be paid (as distinguished from a salary)
fraud	forms of financial investment
outgoings	money given for services rendered (e.g. in a restaurant or bar)
pocket money	money returned to a payer
refund	practice of funding a project or venture by raising monetary contributions from a large number of people
slot machine	spending money given to a child
tip	the opposite of income, i.e. money you spend on bills, household items etc.

18

application	buying or selling securities or commodities
company profile	estimate of cost
jack of all trades	request for employment or admission to a school/college
night shift	salary in relation to how well you carry out responsibilities at work
overtime	sketch/analysis representing the extent to which a company exhibits various characteristics
performance-related pay	someone who can conduct any kind of (manual) job
quote	very good job in high position
start up	very new enterprise/company
top job	work done in addition to regular working hours
trading	working period that takes place at night typically in manual jobs but also in hospitals

19-22 Verbs

19

blast	change task/job frequently and only do the job rather superficially
blush	laugh quietly or with restraint
bury	move smoothly and effortlessly
chuckle	negotiate over a price, terms of an agreement
flit	place a dead person in a grave
fret	play games for money; take a risk in the hope of a favorable outcome

Appendix 2

gamble	play music at a very high volume
glide	travel by getting a free ride from someone
haggle	when your face turns red in embarrassment or shame
hitch	worry

20

peak	abuse vocally by deriding, mocking or criticizing
retire	affect on an emotional or intellectual level
shun	consent reluctantly
spot	deliberately avoid
stare	notice, identify
succumb	stop working because you have reached a certain age
taunt	to reach the highest point; attain maximum intensity
touch	watch/observe in a fixed manner

21

accomplish	attribute the responsibility to someone for something that has gone wrong
aid	be equivalent, similar, equal, or analogous to something else
allure	come to terms or deal successfully with
blame	damage irreparably
cope	declare untrue
decline	entice or attract through personal charm
defy	gain with effort
deny	go against
destroy	help
energize	increase; make better or more attractive
enhance	inject with energy
entail	involve
equate	refuse politely

22

lack	accept as a challenge and deal with
long for	be concerned and bothered with or about something or somebody
mind	do what someone tells you to do
obey	be without
praise	compliment someone who has done something of merit
procrastinate	count on, exploit
rely on	desire strongly or persistently
struggle	desire, want badly
tackle	express an intention that is likely to go against the wishes of the person receiving the threat
tease	have great difficulty
threaten	need and enjoy
thrive	postpone doing what you should be doing
yearn	ridicule, harass, provoke

23-25 Phrasal Verbs and Expressions

23

check up on	end
cheer yourself up	disappoint, make sad/depressed
crop up	have a good relationship with
cut off	investigate, verify
get away with	make yourself feel happier after a negative event
get by	manage to do something without any of the foreseen negative consequences
get on well with	manage, succeed
get rid of	remove; eliminate
get someone down	take place, occur, happen

24

keep something back	allow yourself to be in a weak position so that someone else can potentially do something negative to you
let yourself go	allow yourself to lose your inhibitions
put up with something	be present at
set something aside	cope with or manage some kind of adverse situation without actually trying to change it
set yourself up	reprimand
show up for	put to one side; out of the way (especially away from one's thoughts)
sit out	refrain from mentioning
tell someone off	remain for the whole duration

25

ask someone out	reveal itself to be
bounce back	clean the dishes
cast one's vote	continue on a course of action without being tempted to give up
come out on top	create a state of agitation or an angry disturbance
create a fuss	find
flag someone down	find out whether someone is interested in having a relationship by asking them if they would like to go out for a drink, go to the cinema with you etc.
fool yourself	get very good results, better than others
hang on to	give yourself the wrong impression
hold down a job	keep
risk your shirt	keep your job
stick to something	let another person do whatever he/she wants even though this goes totally against your own best interests
trample over someone	officially express your preference for a particular candidate or option
turn out	return to normality after some negative event
wash up	stand at a roadside attempting to stop a passing car in order to be helped
work out	undertake a venture without regard to possible loss or injury

Appendix 2

Key to Exercises

1

demure	affectedly modest or shy especially in a playful or provocative way
sensitive	being susceptible to attitudes, feelings, or circumstances
idealistic	believing in some (possibly unattainable) morals, values and principles
deluded	believing that you have a particular quality when in fact you probably don't
obnoxious	causing disapproval or protest
selfless	concerned for the welfare of others rather than your own needs
selfish	concerned only with yourself to the exclusion of others
proud	feeling good about someone close (partner, member of family, colleague) due to their very good performance

2

guilty	feeling responsible for something that you have done (or not done)
resentful	full of resentment and ill will
introspective	given to examining your sensory and perceptual experiences
resigned	having come to accept
wise	having good judgment or common sense in practical matters often (but not necessarily) acquired in later life
gentle	having or showing a kindly or tender nature
ineffectual	lacking in power or forcefulness
dull	lacking in liveliness or interest

3

reckless	marked by defiant disregard for danger or consequences
intuitive	obtained through intuition rather than from reasoning or observation
pushy	rather aggressive ambition
open-minded	ready to entertain new ideas
moronic	ridiculous
fulfilled	satisfied
loyal	showing constant support for a person

4

obsessed	showing excessive or compulsive concern with something
sensible	showing reason or sound judgment
prying	too curious or inquisitive
discreet	unobtrusive
miserable	very unhappy
submissive	willing to submit to orders or wishes of others
bulldozing	aggressive

5

annoyed	bothered by petty annoyances
bedraggled	in a very bad condition
bloated	with a very full stomach

captivated	filled with wonder and delight
discredited	no longer accepted; brought into disrepute
flustered	thrown into a state of agitated confusion
folded	with your arms placed inside each other
hard wired	genetically determined
impeded	made difficult or slow
irritated	aroused to impatience or anger
overqualified	with more than a sufficient number of qualifications and thus probably unsuitable/unsuited to a particular job
unscathed	completely unharmed

6

addictive	making you unable to stop (typically of a bad habit)
bitter	marked by strong resentment or cynicism
buzzing	noisy like the sound of a bee
challenging	requiring full use of your abilities or resources
cheery	bright and pleasant; promoting a feeling of cheer
compatible	able to exist and perform in harmonious or agreeable combination
dreadful	exceptionally bad or displeasing
exotic	characteristic of another (apparently more exciting) place or part of the world
resourceful	requiring full use of your abilities or resources

7

foul	unpleasant
hideous	extremely ugly
intriguing	capable of arousing interest or curiosity
lovely	beautiful, very nice
pointless	serving no useful purpose
straightforward	direct, free from ambiguity
tidy	marked by good order and cleanliness in appearance or habits
trendy	in accord with the latest fashion
yummy	extremely pleasing to the sense of taste

8

back of your mind (be at the)	a feeling or thought that is constantly with you
be better off	be in a better position/situation
be dealt a bad hand	be given a series of negative factors to deal with
bear a grudge	maintain resentment or anger against someone for a past offense
bright side of life (look on the)	always see the positive aspects of a situation
call into question	dispute the subject matter at issue
cut corners	not complete tasks as they should be, not act in a proper way
do your bit	make your contribution
face up to	address a problem and try to deal with it
fair amount	adequate; considerable quantity

Appendix 2

9

fill someone with delight	provide a feeling of extreme pleasure or satisfaction
give credit when credit is due	recognize an achievement when it deserves praise
go into the red	go under the permitted amount on your bank account
go too far	go beyond a norm in opinion or actions
jump to conclusions	decide something very quickly without reasoning about it
just for the hell of it	just for fun
keep your cool	maintain your calm in a difficult situation
lend a sympathetic ear	listen to someone with understanding and compassion
make the grade	be of a sufficiently high standard
play sick	pretend to be ill in order not to have to do something that you don't want to do
pour your heart out	tell someone your deepest feelings in a prolonged spurt

10

practice what you preach	act in accordance with how you say that you should act
put yourself in someone else's shoes	project yourself into someone else's predicament and understand how they feel
say what's on your mind	express what you really think about something
the end justifies the means	a good outcome excuses any wrongs committed to achieve it
think outside the box	not to think in the usual standard way, but instead think laterally in order generate unusual approaches or solutions
top of the range	the best in its category
turn out right	have a final positive result
turn your hand at something	be able to conduct a manual task or a job
work out right	have a final positive result

11

take a stand against	oppose
take something to heart	take criticism seriously and be affected or upset by it
take something to the next level	progress to a higher and better point/stage
take the initiative	show readiness to embark on new ventures
take time off	stop going to work for a limited period

12

addiction	an abnormally strong desire due to being dependent on something that is psychologically or physically habit-forming
advice	a proposal for an appropriate course of action

argument	heated discussion (i.e. where there is strong disagreement)
autonomy	independence
awareness	inner knowledge
comfort zone	a situation where you feel safe and at ease
critical thinking	the process of using your mind to consider something carefully
dare	a challenge to do something dangerous
drama	a highly (and probably unnecessarily) emotional episode

13

gossip	light informal (but potentially malicious) conversation for social occasions
humility	the opposite of arrogance
intuition	instinctive knowing without the use of rational processes
merit	admirable quality or attribute
panic	overcome by a sudden fear
perfectionism	a disposition to feel that anything less than perfect is unacceptable
praise	expression of approval and commendation
prestige	a high standing achieved through success
ruin	an irrecoverable state of destruction

14

self esteem	an attitude of admiration, approval and liking of and for oneself
shame	a painful emotion resulting from an awareness of inadequacy
shyness	a feeling of fear of embarrassment
spice	something more interesting than what is currently available
sympathy	sharing and understanding the negative feelings or situation of others
trait	a distinguishing feature of your personal nature
trouble	in a bad situation that you have created yourself
wellbeing	a contented state of being happy, healthy and prosperous
white lie	a statement (considered of no great importance) that deviates from the truth

15

beggar	a poor person who lives by asking people in the street for money or food
broadcaster	someone who transmits a program or some information on radio or television
butcher	a person who slaughters meat for market; someone who sells meat from a shop
civil servant	a person working in the public administration
croupier	someone who collects and pays bets at a gaming table
entrepreneur	someone who organizes a business venture and assumes the risk for it
firefighter	a member of a fire department who tries to extinguish fires
human resources manager	someone in charge of a group of team of people that recruits, interviews, and trains employees as well as dealing with their individual issues
midwife	a woman skilled in aiding the delivery of babies

Appendix 2   159

16

pensioner	someone who is no longer in employment and who receives money (a pension) from the state
plumber	person who installs and repairs pipes and fixtures and appliances
stall-holder	someone with a vending point at a market
surgeon	a physician who specializes in surgery, i.e. cutting open the human body to perform a medical intervention
teller	an employee of a bank who receives and pays out money
tradesman	a merchant who owns or manages a shop
vegan	someone who eats no animal or dairy products at all
workaholic	person with a compulsive need to work

17

bargain	an advantageous purchase
bonds, stocks, shares	forms of financial investment
charity	an institution set up to provide help to the needy; a foundation created to promote the public good
commission	fee for services rendered based on a percentage of an amount received or collected or agreed to be paid (as distinguished from a salary)
crowdfunding	practice of funding a project or venture by raising monetary contributions from a large number of people
fixed rate deal	amount of a charge or payment that is established at the beginning of a job to be done and which binds the party providing the service
fraud	deliberate dishonest behavior intended to gain an advantage
outgoings	the opposite of income, i.e. money you spend on bills, household items etc.
pocket money	spending money given to a child
refund	money returned to a payer
slot machine	a machine for gambling typical found in bars, cinemas etc.
tip	money given for services rendered (e.g. in a restaurant or bar)

18

application	request for employment or admission to a school/college
company profile	sketch/analysis representing the extent to which a company exhibits various characteristics
jack of all trades	someone who can conduct any kind of (manual) job
night shift	working period that takes place at night typically in manual jobs but also in hospitals
overtime	work done in addition to regular working hours
performance-related pay	salary in relation to how well you carry out responsibilities at work
quote	estimate of cost
start up	very new enterprise/company
top job	very good job in high position
trading	buying or selling securities or commodities

19

blast	play music at a very high volume
blush	when your face turns red in embarrassment or shame
bury	place a dead person in a grave
chuckle	laugh quietly or with restraint
flit	change task/job frequently and only do the job rather superficially
fret	worry
gamble	play games for money; take a risk in the hope of a favorable outcome
glide	move smoothly and effortlessly
haggle	negotiate over a price, terms of an agreement
hitch	travel by getting a free ride from someone

20

peak	to reach the highest point; attain maximum intensity
retire	stop working because you have reached a certain age
shun	deliberately avoid
spot	notice, identify
stare	watch/observe in a fixed manner
succumb	consent reluctantly
taunt	abuse vocally by deriding, mocking or criticizing
touch	affect on an emotional or intellectual level

21

accomplish	gain with effort
aid	help
allure	entice or attract through personal charm
blame	attribute the responsibility to someone for something that has gone wrong
cope	come to terms or deal successfully with
decline	refuse politely
defy	go against
deny	declare untrue
destroy	damage irreparably
energize	inject with energy
enhance	increase; make better or more attractive
entail	involve
equate	be equivalent, similar, equal, or analogous to something else

22

lack	be without
long for	desire strongly or persistently
mind	be concerned and bothered with or about something or somebody
obey	be obedient to
praise	compliment someone who has done something of merit
procrastinate	postpone doing what you should be doing

Appendix 2

rely on	count on, exploit
struggle	have great difficulty
tackle	accept as a challenge and deal with
tease	ridicule, harass, provoke
threaten	express an intention that is likely to go against the wishes of the person receiving the threat
thrive	need and enjoy
yearn	desire, want badly

23

check up on	investigate, verify
cheer yourself up	make yourself feel happier after a negative event
crop up	take place, occur, happen
cut off	end
get away with	manage to do something without any of the foreseen negative consequences
get by	manage, succeed
get on well with	have a good relationship with
get rid of	remove; eliminate
get someone down	disappoint, make sad/depressed

24

keep something back	refrain from mentioning
let yourself go	allow yourself to lose your inhibitions
put up with something	cope with or manage some kind of adverse situation without actually trying to change it
set something aside	put to one side; out of the way (especially away from one's thoughts)
set yourself up	allow yourself to be in a weak position so that someone else can potentially do something negative to you
show up for	be present at
sit out	remain for the whole duration
tell someone off	reprimand

25

ask someone out	find out whether someone is interested in having a relationship by asking them if they would like to go out for a drink, go to the cinema with you etc.
bounce back	return to normality after some negative event
cast one's vote	officially express your preference for a particular candidate or option
come out on top	get very good results, better than others
create a fuss	create a state of agitation or an angry disturbance
flag someone down	stand at a roadside attempting to stop a passing car in order to be helped
fool yourself	give yourself the wrong impression
hang on to	keep
hold down a job	keep your job

risk your shirt	undertake a venture without regard to possible loss or injury
stick to something	continue on a course of action without being tempted to give up
trample over someone	let another person do whatever he/she wants even though this goes totally against your own best interests
turn out	reveal itself to be
wash up	clean the dishes
work out	find

Index

Note: The numbers in this index refer to the number of the personality test.

A
Air passenger, 61
Altruistic, 18
Ambition, 21, 27
Assertive, 11
Attention seeking, 15

B
Body, happy with, 24
Boss, 54, 55

C
Cautious, 8
Communicative, 29
Confident, 14

D
Daily habits, 57
Driving, drivers, 29

E
Embarrassed, 12
Ethical, 51, 53
Extrovert, 2

F
Family, 35, 36
Finances, managing, 41
Friend, 32

H
Happy, 23
Health, 22
Honest, 17

I
Image, 27
Imaginative, 28
Internet, 59
Introvert, 1

J
Job, 25, 42–46

L
Left brain, right brain, 38
Logical thinker, 37, 38
Love, 33, 34

M
Managerial potential, 52, 56
Maturity, 58
Meeting skills, 47
Morning or evening, 5

N
Negotiating skills, 48
Nice, 19

P
Parent, 35
Partner, 33, 34
Psychic, 30

R
Responsible, 40
Risk taker, 6, 50

S
Sensation seeker, 7
Shopping, 60

Spontaneous, 9
Stress, 26
Strong character, 13
Supernatural, 30

T
Tactful, 20
Time management, 49
Travel, 29, 61
Trusting, trustworthy, 16

V
Versatile, 39
Victim, 4, 26
Victor, 3

W
Work, 42–56

The manufacturer's authorised representative in the EU is Springer Nature Customer Service Centre GmbH, Europaplatz 3, 69115 Heidelberg, Germany. If you have any concerns regarding our products, please contact ProductSafety@springernature.com

Printed and bound by CPI Group (UK) Ltd, Croydon, CR0 4YY

23/03/2026

02076675-0018